PRAISE FOR *ALIGNMENT*

"Chuck Parry is a wonderful gift to our Bethel community. His affection for God and his childlike faith have caused many impossibilities to bow to the name of Jesus. His new book, *Alignment,* puts into words the truths we see Chuck live out every day with great hope, simple faith, and contagious joy. And from that place of friendship with God, he demonstrates his love for the Holy Spirit and people. I encourage you to read this book and feed your soul. In doing so, you will no doubt fall in love with Jesus all over again and be equipped to invade the impossible in His name."

BILL JOHNSON
Senior Leader of Bethel Church, Redding, California
Author of *The Way of Life* and *Raising Giant-Killers*

"In his book *Alignment*, Chuck Parry stirs faith for the impossible to become a natural outworking of our relationship with Jesus. Chuck's insights, revelatory soundbites, and incredible accounts of God breaking into people's lives are simply breathtaking. In this book you will get to discover what our union with Jesus really means and how our right understanding and believing work to unlock the same empowered life that Jesus enjoyed. What I love about Chuck is that he is able to unlock supernatural life in an authentic, vulnerable way. He not only gives you theological truths to build your life on; he also gives you some of his internal dialogue and process that will empower you to actually step out into a life of revealing God's heart to the broken and hurting world around you. Reading this book has once again stirred me to live out of who I am in Jesus and to align myself with Heaven rather than trying to perform or work hard at doing 'the Kingdom stuff.' *Alignment* will do just that for you as you read this book; it will connect you and align you to the great destiny that comes from our shared life with Christ."

JULIAN ADAMS
Director of Frequentsee
Author of *The Kiss of the Father*
and internationally known prophetic minister

"Chuck is the 'real deal.' He lives what he preaches. I am honored to walk side by side with this man of God. You will be amazed and touched by his stories of both connection to God and the miracles he has seen because of this great connection."

DAWNA DE SILVA
Founder and co-leader of Bethel Church Sozo
Author of the books *Sozo, Shifting Atmospheres,* and *Overcoming Fear*

"Get your highlighter ready for a read that's dense with truth and life. Chuck has a gift for making the spiritual so practical you'll walk away with a Holy Spirit rush every time you pick it up. His first book, *Free-Falling,* rocked my world, instilling a new confidence to know that I can free-fall and land on my feet. I wanted more. *Alignment* may be Chuck Parry's magnum opus. He walks forward like Jesus in all his stories, dispelling lies and dispersing truth. This book lights my path and charges my world with Holy Spirit electricity like a lightning bolt from Heaven displaying God's glory as it dispels the devil's lies we all too often believe to be commonplace. 'Just as darkness is not an entity on its own, but rather the absence of light, so the lie is not a living entity, but rather the intentional absence of Truth. And when we agree with any lie we step outside the realm of His perfection into places of distortion in our thinking.' Chuck is handing me the broom I need to sweep all the junk out of my mind. But he doesn't stop there. He goes on to replace all the junk with a unique understanding of God's nature that fills every crevice in my heart, threading a constant reminder throughout to hold onto God's promises and our faith, against all odds. This book will be sitting next to my Bible. Forever thank you, Chuck!"

LINDSEY CLIFFORD
Writer

"What a joy plus honor to scream out loud the benefits of Chuck Parry's remarkable new book. Chuck's *Free-Falling* brought a new spiritual, practical, full-of-Joy perspective to my life, and now this book takes it further. Tell everyone you know that Chuck is in the house and that the man of God has spoken!"

DR. MICHAEL K. CLIFFORD
Entrepreneur

ALIGNMENT

ALIGNMENT

LIVE A LIFE OF MIRACLES

CHUCK PARRY

SALEM
BOOKS
an imprint of Regnery Publishing

Scriptures marked AMP are taken from the AMPLIFIED® BIBLE. Copyright © 1954, 1958, 1962, 1964, 1965, 1987 by the Lockman Foundation (www.Lockman.org). Used by permission.

Scriptures marked AMPC are taken from the AMPLIFIED BIBLE, CLASSIC EDITION. Copyright © 1954, 1958, 1962, 1964, 1965, 1987 by the Lockman Foundation (www.Lockman.org). Used by permission.

Scriptures marked ERV are taken from the Holy Bible: Easy-to-Read Version (ERV), International Edition. Copyright © 2013, 2016 by Bible League International. Used by permission.

Scriptures marked ESV are taken from THE HOLY BIBLE, ENGLISH STANDARD VERSION®. Copyright © 2001 by Crossway, a publishing ministry of Good News Publishers. Used by permission.

Scriptures marked KJV are taken from the KING JAMES VERSION, public domain.

Scriptures marked MEV are taken from the Modern English Version. Copyright © 2014 by Military Bible Association. Used by permission. All rights reserved.

Scriptures marked MSG are taken from THE MESSAGE: THE BIBLE IN CONTEMPORARY ENGLISH. Copyright © 1993, 1994, 1995, 1996, 2000, 2001, 2002. Used by permission of NavPress Publishing Group.

Scriptures marked NASB are taken from the NEW AMERICAN STANDARD BIBLE®. Copyright © 1960, 1962, 1963, 1968, 1971, 1972, 1973, 1975, 1977, 1995 by the Lockman Foundation. Used by permission.

Scriptures marked NIV are taken from THE HOLY BIBLE, NEW INTERNATIONAL VERSION®. Copyright © 1973, 1978, 1984, 2011 by Biblica, Inc.™. Used by permission of Zondervan.

Scriptures marked NKJV are taken from the NEW KING JAMES VERSION®. Copyright © 1982 by Thomas Nelson, Inc. Used by permission. All rights reserved.

Scriptures marked NLT are taken from THE HOLY BIBLE, NEW LIVING TRANSLATION (NLT). Copyright © 1996, 2004, 2007 by Tyndale House Foundation. Used by permission of Tyndale House Publishers, Inc., Carol Stream, Illinois, 60188. All rights reserved. Used by permission.

Scripture quotations marked TPT are from The Passion Translation®. Copyright © 2017, 2018 by Passion & Fire Ministries, Inc. (ThePassionTranslation.com). Used by permission. All rights reserved.

Salem Books™ is a trademark of Salem Communications Holding Corporation
Regnery® is a registered trademark of Salem Communications Holding Corporation

ISBN: 978-1-68451-081-8
eISBN: 978-1-68451-093-1

Library of Congress Control Number: 2019956676

Published in the United States by
Salem Books
An imprint of Regnery Publishing
A division of Salem Media Group
300 New Jersey Ave NW
Washington, DC 20001
www.Regnery.com

Manufactured in the United States of America

10 9 8 7 6 5 4 3 2 1

Books are available in quantity for promotional or premium use. For information on discounts and terms, please visit our website: www.Regnery.com.

Contents

Foreword

I met Chuck Parry some years ago when he first visited us in West Sussex in the UK. In our churches, we were hungry and committed, seeking to see signs and wonders become a normal part of our proclamation of the Gospel of the Kingdom. What we read in the scriptures of the life of Jesus and the early Church was not our daily experience. We needed some help. So I invited Chuck to lead us into discovery of a life of regular miracles. Yet what we received was so much more …

Chuck lifted us into an ongoing, ever-increasing experience of life lived within what I can only describe as the *Trinitarian love-symphony of God*. He showed us this is the realm we are invited to inhabit through Jesus Christ. In fact, we have never *not* inhabited it—we just never knew how much He had won, and how wonderful He really is! We have discovered a reality of Father, Son, and Spirit where all earthly limitations are released, unending glory is found, and all lost things made new.

Having known a little of Chuck's ministry from afar, I felt it might be something of a risk to invite him to us. As English people, we are raised in a culture that often celebrates a "natural" British reserve. On a bad day, we are perhaps quite cautious of American positivity and what we often perceive as excessive enthusiasm. Add into the mix historically controversial topics like supernatural healing, and it is fair to say I was not entirely sure how Chuck would go down … or how far I would go down as a result!

But I underestimated the sensitivity of the man and leader that he is. With precision and skill, he laid the biblical foundations he immediately sensed that we needed. With consistent love and an infectious joy, he disarmed our seriousness and overcame our fear. Looking back over several years and the various trips and visits he has made to us, I can say with a genuine sense of awe that I—and we, and many British church leaders who have joined us—have been utterly transformed by God in and through Chuck Parry.

To be around Chuck—whether in conference mode, on a Face-Time call, or over a meal—is to be drawn into the atmosphere of Heaven. When you are with him, the room becomes lighter, joy begins to infuse everything, burdens slip away, and problems diminish in size. I couldn't understand why he kept laughing when I first spent time with him. After a while, I began to realize how little I laughed …

You see, what Chuck broke in me was a sense of drivenness, a sense that I would need to work really hard to achieve break-through and to flourish. He showed me that this beautiful activity of the Kingdom is not gained through dogged perseverance but through simply recognising the full work of Christ and abiding in Him. This is a man who lives connected to God—aligned—and, as a result, Heaven comes down through him. This is his real secret, and I am so thankful he has shared it with us.

And then I began to see how theologically and biblically skilled he is. Chuck lives the most thrilling unity of Word and Spirit that I have observed: Everything he is and says is grounded in deep scriptural revelation and reflection, yet at the same time, he models and demonstrates everything to create explosive spiritual encounter. If you are looking for line-by-line biblical exposition, he can exhilaratingly do it—but get ready to be catapulted into the experiential truth of what he is teaching.

Reading this book has felt to me like a literary version of authentic Chuck Parry: He shares story after story of God's goodness before revealing something about God that is completely new. He does this in a way that makes you feel like you've always known it deep down but never quite dared believe it. When he is ministering, he will then step back with complete humility, and to avoid you ever thinking he is the superstar miracle worker, he will release everyone to "have a go." One of my favourite moments of one of Chuck's visits with us was when an eighteen-year-old young man joined in when the young people were releasing healing during a meeting. This lad saw multiple healing miracles through his own hands that night. It wasn't until a week later that he gave his life to Christ!

I can confidently verify the life-changing dynamic of some of the revelation in this book. We have been transformed by "blue sky at the beach," learning the atmosphere-shifting power of thanksgiving and our delegated authority in creation. We love to partner with Father in prophetic acts and are having so much fun releasing healing to precious people in body, mind, and spirit. Miracles are regularly in evidence amongst our people wherever they go, and a material fruit of Chuck's inspiration and investment in us has seen the birthing of the Chanctonbury Healing Centre. As Rector, it brings me so much joy to hear countless stories of forever-changed lives as salvation, healing, deliverance, and freedom are powerfully and lovingly released by our lion-like healing team. Chuck has given us the confidence and imparted grace to our communities to run with this.

But perhaps what I have valued the most is the rich, humble, deep, and extravagant love that Chuck has poured out to us, and to me. When we first met, he saw my underlying mentality of performance and fear, and loved me into joy and freedom. His encouragement and friendship have constantly championed me to believe Heaven is truly the limit! He has never demanded, expected, or pushed. He is the same off-stage as he is on the microphone, and he has won the hearts of our communities through constant patience, kindness, generosity, and impeccable integrity.

It is an honour to count him as a friend and father to all God is pouring out in our midst. I pray this book will release the inexhaustible riches of Christ in you that Chuck has released in us.

Rev. James di Castiglione
Rector, Chanctonbury Churches
West Sussex, Church of England

Introduction

I was in a room full of people and, looking around, spotted a young man to whom I felt an immediate attraction. "What attracts You to this man?" I asked God. Suddenly, I saw a movie in my mind of him playing baseball and saw a father in the stands shouting louder than anyone else. Feeling the Father's love well up in me for this young hero, I took a risk and stepped out in the overflow of that love.

"Excuse me, my name is Chuck, and when I looked at you I saw a movie go through my mind with you in it. Can I share that image with you?" I've found that everyone is interested in the movie in which they are the star!

He agreed, and I went on: "I saw you playing baseball, and I felt the Father's heart well up with pride over you. Then I heard Him shouting out from the stands, and He was that loud, obnoxious guy who shouted louder than anyone else: 'Whose boy is that? Yeah, whose boy is that? Yeah, that's *my* boy!' He shouted again and again with pride. The Father wants you to know that you are the son He loves; His pride and delight are in you. He's your biggest fan! He comes to all your games; He's never missed one. He's so proud of you. He's proud of you when you score, and He's proud of you when you fall down and get back up again. He's proud of you just because you're His, because you're His son."

Tears welled up in the young man's eyes, and he wept while I hugged him, wrapped him in my arms, and poured the Father's blessing into and all over him. When we parted, I asked him what that meant to him.

"I was a professional baseball player," he said. "My father did come to my games, and he *was* that loud, obnoxious guy who yelled louder than anyone—only he always cursed me out, called me an idiot, criticized every play, and constantly shouted his disapproval and disdain. What you said pierced right to that place I've tried to forget, but it comes up again and again. Somehow, God went in right now and touched that place with His Father love, filled me up, and suddenly everything is different." *Oh Jesus, thank You! You make all things new.*

Where did that movie in my mind originate? So often we'll think, *That's just my imagination.* I believe the imagination is like the computer monitor of our inner realm. We dream, create, design and visualize on its screen. It's the place where our invisible parts— our mind, soul, and spirit—find a venue to express the endless ideas, inventions, and creativity that long to manifest in the physical realm.

And because we share this body, this temple, this tabernacle with another, we see that other One expressing ideas and creativity on our screen as well. The Holy Spirit, Spirit of the Living God, Creator of the universe and Spirit of Him who raised Jesus from the dead, lives in me.[1] That's what He tells me in His word, the Bible. He has dreams, designs, plans. So it is no longer a question of "Is it just my imagination … ?" but rather, "Who is visualizing here, who initiated this one, and how are we interacting with this idea, dream, or concept that is on the screen right now?"

I had an inspiration while I was reading about the baptism of Jesus in the gospels. The heavens were ripped open, the affirmation of the Father boomed forth over the Son He loves, and the Holy Spirit landed upon Him—the Son standing on the earth, receiving everything the Father and the Spirit sent Him from Heaven. I saw in my mind a plumb line drop from Heaven to the Son on earth as if He were the center of gravity, that source of energy that pulled all the magnetic force of Heaven to itself. Who projected this image on the computer screen of my mind? And when I'm praying for someone for a miracle of healing and I see that plumb line dropping from God to the center of gravity of the Son in me, touching that person's need, and I watch his symptoms leave and the Now of Heaven come with power, who projected that picture into my imagination? Sometimes, I know it's God who initiates. But when I remember something He once initiated, am I "trying to visualize, trying to make something happen"— or simply agreeing with something He has previously shown me is very real and powerful?

This book is about learning to interact with the God who lives within us and see alignment with all the capacity of Heaven come. It's about connecting with His heart for that baseball player, that person who has cancer, that lonely wounded person, that empty bank account, or that earthly problem that longs for a solution, and seeing Heaven open up for them. It's about experimenting with "doing what I see the Father doing …"[2] It's about being a son, and it's about the adventures …

Chuck Parry
Redding, California
May 2020

plumb line:

noun. a line directed to the center of gravity of the earth; a vertical line; a string with a metal weight at one end—when suspended, it points directly towards the earth's center of gravity and so is used to check that vertical structures are true

used symbolically, it refers to the divine standard against which God, the builder of his people, tests and judges them; it also symbolizes the standard by which God rebuilds his people

Amos 7:7–8; 9:11–15; Isaiah 28:17a. NIV

plumb:
adj. exactly vertical or true, standing perfectly upright, not leaning in any way

verb. to examine (a thing) in a careful and complete way so as to understand it:
a. to a complete degree—*absolutely*
b. in a direct manner—*exactly*
c. without interval of time—*immediately*

CHAPTER 1

THE
IMMEDIATELY
OF GOD

"It is time for the realm of God's Kingdom to be experienced in its fullness!"
—JESUS[1]

She was eighty-four years old when she came into the Healing Rooms at Bethel Church, asking for prayer for relief from the back pain she was experiencing. Noticing that she limped and her right arm hung loosely at her side, we learned she'd had polio as a baby and her right leg and arm had never fully developed. They were shorter than her left limbs, and the joints didn't work properly. She'd lived with them for eighty-four years and was bright and cheerful, clearly an overcomer.

A nine-year-old boy from our Children's Team approached and, looking at her, said, "Your leg is too short." (No filters on that child!) She explained to him about polio, and he simply replied: "Can we grow it out?" She had never considered that, but she gave consent, and he had her sit in a chair while he held her two feet

1

out, above the floor, and said: "Grow!" To her absolute surprise, the leg shot out a few inches, which she definitely felt. As she stood on the new leg, she was dumbfounded by the change in her stature and balance, as well as the fact that her hip, knee, and ankle seemed to work! The team cheered and celebrated, and I asked her if there was anything she was unable to do before that perhaps she could now do. She had never walked up and down stairs in a normal fashion.

"We have stairs right out in the hallway!" I exclaimed. "Would you like to go out and try them?"

She mounted the stairs gracefully and then turned around. I got to see her face as, for the first time in eighty-four years, she walked down stairs with her hip, knee, and ankle all functioning in perfection, completely free from pain! She was awestruck! I escorted her to the table where our team writes down the stories of healing that happen that day, introduced her, and she proceeded to describe her condition.

When I passed by about ten minutes later, she stopped me. "Look at this. I've never done this in my entire life," she stated as she picked up a water bottle in her right hand and swung it over her head. She marveled as she explored all her new working parts. Eighty-four years! Suddenly, her whole life was different.

When I see such dramatic and instantaneous transformations, I often think about what must have occurred in the heavenly realms to allow these wonders to happen. I often study the life of Jesus to watch and learn what He accomplished that opened up for us the access to this grace wherein we live and move and have our being. How did He bring about this open Heaven wherein we stand under the outpouring of God's love and see things instantly change? Is it God's plan for man to stand in such abundance of grace, in such a gift of righteousness that we can see Him doing wondrous things in our midst and be so honored and favored that He would use us, and even a young boy, as He accomplishes these miracles?

I found answers to these questions as I was reading the Gospel of Mark one day.

THE PLUMB LINE OF HEAVEN

John the crazy man came out of the wild places with fire in his eyes and a brilliance about him that came from the burning passion in his spirit and overflowed until it filled all the atmosphere around him. His wiry, sun-darkened body was covered in camel hide, and he ate—really—crunchy locusts and sticky-sweet wild honey. His words bore a weight that caused everyone to take note until they could no longer measure themselves by any other standard than the plumb line of God. This required some adjusting, and he offered the solution: "Repent, for the Kingdom of Heaven is here!" He came as a witness that the Light of the World was among us and we needed to prepare ourselves for Him. There was a baptism—an immersion—into a repentance, or turning of the whole direction of our focus toward God, that brought a remission or complete removal of our sins, a wonderful cleansing from all the guilt and shame and punishment, and a full restoration into the glorious freedom of the children of God. Wow!

The people went out to him in droves, and he put them under the rushing current of the river to come up somehow wonderfully clean and changed, aligned with the plumb line of Heaven. It was the call on his life, his destiny. He was the voice in the wilderness crying out: "Prepare the Way of the Lord; make His paths straight."

And then Jesus came like an alien from Heaven, His feet in the dust of the earth, but His heart and mind connected and pulling on the unseen realm. And John saw Him, and John recognized Him. Jesus, the Holy One, the Lamb of God, stepped into the river, and John put Him under, but not without protesting, "Who am I, Lord … ?"

Immediately as He came up through the surface of the moving water, the heavens were ripped open, and The Voice boomed out from an unseen source: "You are My beloved Son; in You I am well pleased." And the Holy Spirit of God came upon Him in a form all could see: a dove who stayed on this One, the son of man who was being revealed as the Son of God.

And "*immediately* the Spirit drove Him into the wilderness …" That word keeps showing up in the Gospel of Mark—twelve times in the first chapter alone. Curiously, it's the same word used for "straight" in John's charge to the people to make a direct route for the coming of the One. It's the immediately of God, when we align with Heaven and the favor of God blows open the skies and His Glory fires down on us and seals us as His own, a child of Heaven and son or daughter of the Living God.

Immediately in the Greek manuscripts is εὐθέως *(eutheōs)*, which means "immediately, directly, straightway,"[2] and is used nine times in the first chapter of Mark. Three more times in the same chapter, its root word, εὐθύς *(euthys)* is used to mean "immediately and straightway" but also "a straight way, one that is plumb or level, right, and also straightforward, upright, true, sincere."[3]

When we stand under that same Open Heaven as true sons and daughters, in Christ as He is in us, all our sins and failures cleansed by Him—aligned with the Father's pure purpose, accepted, embraced, affirmed—we find ourselves loved with the same love with which the Father loves Jesus His Son.[4] And then the Holy Spirit, the Spirit of the Living God, the Spirit of Holiness and Power, comes upon us and we are in the Son and aligned in the plumb line of God; then unlimited life flows from the Father in an Open Heaven to the Son standing on a ready and receptive earth. This is the immediately of God. This is the alignment that brings all the abundance of the heavenly Kingdom into all the realms of this world. This is what God has accomplished for us and in us.

The people entered into the waters of a baptism of repentance for the remission of sins to get in line with a straight, level, plumb, right, and true path for the Way of the Lord to come from Heaven to Earth. It was drama, a prophetic act choreographed by John, the last of the Old Covenant prophets. It pointed to our immersion into the death, burial, and resurrection of Jesus Christ, as the Apostle Paul tells us in Romans 6.[5] Even in the prophetic act, there is power to enter into the immediately of God, that miraculous realm outside of time where the *now* of God brought complete cleansing even before the chronological death and resurrection of Jesus.[6] *How do You do that, God?*

Jesus walked in the plumb line of God, always attentive to what the Father was saying and doing. He lived in the *now* of God; like a lightning rod, He grounded the limitless abundance of Heaven into circumstances and situations, lives, and even concepts and thought processes on the earth. And *immediately*—throughout his gospel, Mark continues to use this word forty-three times—*immediately*, people were healed and their lives transformed. And Jesus extravagantly invites us to enter into it all, one in Him with the Father, welcome to do the works that He does—and even greater works now that He has gone to the Father[7] and They have sent the promised Holy Spirit to be *in* us and *upon* us.[8] It's phenomenal, this great honor and privilege! That we can now stand *in Him*, in the plumb line of Heaven, in the *now* of God that overrides the ravages of time and anyone's terrible choices and see the *immediately* of God sweep in like a tidal wave, a cleansing storm, a hurricane, and all that is wiped out are the results of sin and "the handwriting of the ordinances that were against us …"[9] The *suddenly* of Heaven comes, and we see sickness and disease flee along with the results of even eighty-four years of polio. And with those diseases go guilt, shame, hopelessness, fear, and depression. With the plumb line of Heaven, with the *immediately* of God, the Kingdom of Heaven comes *now* and takes ground, impacting lives with love, hope, joy, healing, abundance, and New Life as it spreads from person to person, embracing all the realms of this world. This is global take-over at its best ...

"That they all may be one, as You, Father, are in Me, and I in You; that they also may be one in Us, that the world may believe that You sent Me. And the glory which You gave Me I have given them, that they may be one just as We are one: I in them, and You in Me; that they may be made perfect in one, and that the world may know that You have sent Me, and have loved them as You have loved Me."

—JESUS[10]

CHAPTER 2

THE WORKS
OF THE FATHER

"I only do the works that I see the Father doing ..."
—JESUS[1]

They're so subtle, the impressions He gives. I saw her twisted face, and I just wanted to hold it in my hands and love her. That was the impression. Her jaw had been broken when she was six years old, and for eighteen years, her face had bent severely toward her right shoulder, causing extreme pain as she opened her mouth or tried to chew. For eighteen years ...

She was a lovely girl with a face bent at an angle and in almost constant pain. I felt the Father's heart swell within me and His love pour out of me toward the young woman. I cupped my hands around her deformed chin and looked into her eyes with the Father's love. And then it happened. Right beneath my hands, her jaw straightened! It was soundless and smooth, as if He were straightening the finest silk fabric. She gasped, and tears streamed down her face. All the pain was instantly gone! The young woman beside her hugged her, and we celebrated God's goodness together.

And then I sensed His Papa heart just wanting to wrap His huge arms of love around her, and I wanted to bless her.

"May I give you a father's blessing?" I asked. She nodded and slid into my arms as I prayed a blessing of love and favor, delight and joy over her. She convulsed in my embrace, weeping as I continued to hold her. I saw a quick flash of old movies over her, and suddenly I knew it was her own father who had hit her in the tender face when she was only six years old, breaking her jaw. Then there were years of abuse and terror, victimization and heartbreak. I poured out love from my own father's heart all over her. When the sobbing ceased, great peace came and wrapped itself around us like a thick down comforter. Finally, we separated, and she breathed deeply, smiled, and then asked, "Can I tell you what happened as you were praying for me?"

"Please."

"When you blessed me, Jesus took me back through all the events of the past and took away all the terror and the fear, the torment and pain. For the first time in my life I am free!"

Wow! Thank You for letting me be part of what You're doing, God. I'm overwhelmed by Your great love for us, how You take us out of impossible situations and transform us, bringing us into freedom and joy, love and wholeness! Thank You.

THE HEART OF THE FATHER

"I pray for them all to be joined together as one even as You and I, Father, are joined together as one. I pray for them to become one with Us so that the world will recognize that You sent Me. For the very glory You have given to Me I have given them so that they will be joined together as one and experience the same unity that We enjoy. You live fully in Me and now I live fully in them so that they will experience perfect unity, and the world will be convinced that You have sent Me, for they will see that You love each one of them with the same passionate love that You have for Me … I have revealed to them who You are and I will continue to make You even more real to them, so that they may experience the same endless love that You have for Me, for Your love will now live in them, even as I live in them!"

—JESUS[2]

What a marvel, what a wonder! The Almighty God who lives outside of time and space, who lives in endlessness—His eternal glory that abides without beginning or end—this God has chosen to step into time and space and right into His creation to live in us! What do we do with such honor and favor?

I have been meditating on Truth. In this same passage in John 17, Jesus says to the Father, "Sanctify them [set them apart for Yourself, pull them into Your holiness, put Your holiness in them and upon them] in the Truth; Your word is Truth."[3] The things that God says are the Truth. What He says about Himself, about us, about the world, plans, and purposes. About everything. And every place we let His words live in us and define us and our world, we find Truth, as well as glorious freedom. As we continue in, abide in, remain in, dwell in, and stay present with His Truth, we are indeed His, and His Truth makes us free![4]

In His Truth, there is no shadow. Just as darkness is not an entity on its own, but rather the absence of light, so the lie is not a living entity but the intentional absence of Truth. And when we agree with any lie, we step outside the realm of His perfection into places of distortion in our thinking. We begin to operate in areas of deception, and unfortunately, we begin to accept this distortion as the way things are. This is why it is crucial to make sure we are "bringing every thought into captivity to the obedience of Christ"[5] because He is "full of Grace and Truth."[6] We are in a constant state of "renewing our minds"[7] to what is Truth. I ask Him to expose every place a lying thought has gained access so that with intentionality I may replace it with the Truth. Jesus is the Way, the Truth, and the Life, …[8] and Holy Spirit is the Spirit of Truth, who guides us into All Truth.[9] We are admonished to *abide*—that word means to stay present, be here now, remain in this Truth, and ignore every distraction trying to get us to look into the past with regret or the future with anxiety—but stay present in His word, His love, His joy, His Truth, and to let those powerful forces abide in us.

So this is the adventure: we get to meditate on Him, His words, His truth, His love, His joy … living in us! He says we are the Temple of the Holy Spirit and the Holy Spirit lives in us.[10] We have the option of thinking on all of the problems that surround us and are apparently overtaking the world or of focusing on Him-in-us, the answer to the problems of the world, the very "desire of all nations."[11] And we can meditate on these things with power because they are the Truth. There are many things we simply must accept as the Truth because He tells us they are. The humanistic mindset wants to figure it out and decide, to be the judge of what is good and evil, but freedom comes when we accept and agree with what God says is true. I am righteous, I am free, I am loved and accepted in The Beloved.[12] I am who He says I am! I stand in alignment with the Plumb Line of Heaven.

I find that there is an honor in recognizing the things He says. When I say, "Thank You that You choose to live in me," I simply agree with what He says, whether I feel, hear, taste, smell, or see Him. In that simple agreement is an honor, a form of worship. Jesus tells us the Father is looking for those who will worship Him in Spirit and in Truth.[13] When I simply recognize His presence based on Truth ("God, You're already here") and turn my attention to Him-in-me, then thank Him, honor Him for being here always, for moving in and cohabiting this body, it is true worship. The amazing thing is that there are immediate benefits, because in the recognition I find I have access to all He is and does, which I ignore when I believe He is absent, far away, and unreachable. I'm not trying to manipulate Him; rather, I'm agreeing with what He says is true. When I do this, I find that His plan is to give life to my mortal body by His Spirit who lives in me[14] and to live and move in and through me, to empower me to bring His Kingdom into all the spheres of my life, to elevate everywhere I am into a place where His glory is. He "only does wondrous things,"[15] and He wants to do them with me!

> "I have been crucified together with Christ, and it is no longer [just] I who live, but Christ lives in me; and the life which I now live [together with Him] in the flesh I live by faith in the Son of God, who loved me and gave Himself for me."
>
> —PAUL[16]

Or, as The Passion Translation so passionately puts it:

> "My old identity has been co-crucified with Messiah and no longer lives; for the nails of his cross crucified me with him. And now the essence of this new life is no longer mine, for the Anointed One lives his life through me—we live in union as one! My new life is empowered by the faith of the Son of God who loves me so much that he gave himself for me, and dispenses his life into mine!"[17]

HERE'S HOW THIS WORKS

I took a seat in a large auditorium and was introducing myself to the neighbors when the woman behind me told me she knew me.

"You don't know me, but eight months ago, you prayed for my husband and he hasn't been the same since."

"Oh, I hope better," I joked. "Please tell me about it."

"He's spent his life in pain, having a terrible childhood, locked in a room, chased by his mother with a knife. He suffered from severe PTSD as well as other forms of depression and psychosis. He would burst out in rage, and it became so terrible that our family could not sit down at the dinner table together for fear of outbreaks of violence. The four children lived in fear, and after twenty-six years of marriage, I was about finished. He came to the Bethel Healing School last May, but called me to tell me that he was done there, the people were crazy, and he was ready to come home. I asked him to give it one more chance. He told me he went into the auditorium and saw you and decided to ask you to pray for him. You looked him in the eyes and wrapped your arms around him and hugged him. My husband is a big, muscular, angry guy who has never experienced or felt love. But when you hugged him, he felt the love of the Father come into him for the first time ever, and he said, 'It left.' He was wrecked, and he came home a different man. He knows joy, has a normal life, has rebuilt trust with the children. After years of torment, we have had eight months of peace, joy, and family life!"

Oh Jesus, You are magnificent in all Your ways. Thank You for touching that man and letting me be a part of his transformation while I seemingly did nothing but love You and be loved by You until that love overflowed into his love-starved heart. I love Your ways!

MORE WONDERS

For months now, God has been encouraging me almost daily with refreshing news of lives transformed by His goodness and power when I had prayed for someone in the past and apparently seen no visible change. One Saturday morning in our Healing Rooms, a woman experienced complete freedom from years of pain. As she was sharing her story and what God had done that day in her body, she said to me, "A year ago, you prayed for my husband. Do you remember? He suffered from severe PTSD and could not even come into the church building but was curled up in a fetal position outside, and I asked you to come out and pray for him. He immediately experienced a measure of peace, but everything continued to change after we went home. His improvement was so radical he is now leading a men's group and counseling other men suffering from PTSD!"

This is why I believe that every time we pray, something happens. It isn't because we have worked up a mighty faith to believe; it's because the simplest, childlike faith that this is God's idea and His plan is enough to demolish the most immoveable stronghold. We don't even have to see the immediate results, but we can begin celebrating and thanking Him because we know it's who He is and what He does! The more we immerse ourselves in His love for us, become overwhelmed by His beauty and goodness, kindness and closeness, and intoxicated with His passion for bringing us all into glorious wholeness, we become magnets for His miracles to overflow and transform lives. Joy just flows until it becomes a mighty river and we are carried away by it. Look into the wonder and beauty of His plan and see if you can resist the tidal wave of joy-filled revelation that flows from His heart right into you, flushing out every doubt to replace it with outrageous hope. Hope is defined as this: "the confident and joy-filled expectation of good"!

"And now we have run into His heart to hide ourselves in His faithfulness. This is where we find His strength and comfort, for He empowers us to seize what has already been established ahead of time—an unshakeable hope! We have this certain hope like a strong, unbreakable anchor holding our souls to God himself. Our anchor of hope is fastened to the mercy seat which sits in the heavenly realm beyond the sacred threshold, and where Jesus, our forerunner, has gone in before us."

—PAUL[18]

CHAPTER 3

THE WILDERNESS

"Do not conform to the pattern of this world,
but be transformed by the renewing of your mind.
Then you will be able to test and approve what God's will is—
His good, pleasing and perfect will."
—PAUL[1]

What if that famous prophet pointed to you in a great assembly of people and said he had a word from God for you? He calls out your name and phone number, the address of the house where you live; people gasp and cheer—there's no doubt it's you. You rise up, trembling with excitement and expectation, waiting for that word you've been longing for that will unlock your destiny and give you a clear view into your future. Excited? Here it comes:

"God is calling you into the wilderness …"

You remain standing, awkwardly. *Wait, that's it?* What images fill your imagination? As you slide back into your seat, you think of the Israelites wandering in the desert for forty years eating manna and wearing the same clothes and shoes until they die there. *Uh, thanks … Can I get a different word, please?*

The wilderness, the desert. We can think of all the things that make it eminently unappealing. But wait. We are in a constant state of renewing our minds, of learning to think like God, our thoughts influenced by the very *now* experience of Heaven in our midst. How does God see the wilderness? Was it a place of punishment, of dire lack in the midst of hoped-for abundance, a place of stripping and shedding, of fiery trials? Or did He have another plan?

One of my interns shared a dream he had where God showed him the blueprint of his mind. Being a builder, this caught his interest. It was a two-dimensional transparency full of great detail and orderly design. And then God placed a second blueprint over the first. It stretched into multi-dimensions and expanded into multi-layers, an extremely extensive, intricate, beautiful, and complex transparency that God said was His Mind superimposed over my friend's mind. And then it all became clear: we have the Mind of Christ.[2] We have access to the very thought life of Heaven, the creative genius of the imaginer of the universe. His Spirit lives inside us, the Spirit of Truth who leads us into all truth[3] and takes what belongs to Jesus—His wisdom, insight, understanding, creative thinking, the very Mind of Christ—and makes it known to us.[4] That same Holy Spirit lives in us as a deposit guaranteeing the whole inheritance[5] of Jesus, who is the heir of all things.[6] Wait. The deposit on the inheritance ... is Holy Spirit, who is ... God! It's God Himself! He is the access we have to everything, to the Mind of Christ and to "every spiritual blessing in the Heavenly places."[7] *Whoa.*

So this makes me think: *What is God's view of the wilderness? What was His plan when He told Pharaoh, the mightiest king in the world, to let His people go that they might—do what?—in the wilderness? Wait ... Oh, yes: Worship Me in the wilderness.* God's purpose was to deliver millions of His people from slavery to the most powerful entity on earth and bring them to the mountain where they might meet Him face-to-face in all His Goodness, Glory, Holiness, and Terror and worship Him. Where He might bring them into an encounter with the God of all creation right in the midst of the wild, untamed, barren ruggedness of His creation and be with them as a fiery pillar by night and a cloud by day, a real and present God who would fill their real and present needs, a true Provider. He would create of them in that place a New Thing, never before seen: a Nation whose king is the one true, almighty God in the midst of them, a God who is moved and moves on their behalf. He would create a kingdom out of slaves, a nation from a family, and right there in that untamed wilderness, full of raw, elemental danger and the primal unknown, He would be their God and Father, and they would be His people, His family. He would superimpose order and provision and purpose and Presence upon them, and they would be a holy people, a nation whose God is their real and present king, right there among them. What a glorious plan!

From that place, He would lead them into the Land of All His Promises, a rich land that He would give them, a prosperous land of walled cities and farms and vineyards, houses, and barns already built, a fruitful land flowing with abundance: "For the Lord your God is bringing you into a good land—a land with brooks, streams, and deep springs gushing out into the valleys and hills; a land with wheat and barley, vines and fig trees, pomegranates, olive oil and honey; a land where bread will not be scarce and you will lack nothing; a land where the rocks are iron and you can dig copper out of the hills."[8] It was a short trip across the rocky, barren desert to this good land.

In God's mind, a call to the wilderness is a call to encounter Him, to come to Him in all His glory and abundance and be overwhelmed by promise and hope, to taste of the good fruit before you even plant the tree, to see into His mind and heart and be forever changed. Nothing shall ever be impossible again. He's the Almighty God, and I am the son that He loves. I come away from the encounter as a new creation with a fresh vision, and all things are possible.

I am forever changed. And from that place, He leads me into the Land of All His Promises; my destiny becomes enlarged to contain the Divine Plan; "supernatural" is now who I am and the realm in which I live, not simply what I can do. The King and His Kingdom are vibrant within me, ready to explode outward and impact the world around me. And now I am ready to fulfill His purpose: God in me and I in Him. *Lead me into the wilderness again and again and again, Lord.*

We think of the Israelites' trials in the wilderness and of Jesus's own trials in the desert. What does it mean? Jesus moved into a supernatural, heavenly encounter when He approached John at the river and stepped into a baptism. The heavens were ripped open, fulfilling the prophetic heart cry of Isaiah: "Oh that You would rend the heavens and come down, that the mountains might shake at Your Presence … that the nations may tremble …"[9] As the heavens split, the Voice of the Father boomed out His ultimate affirmation: "You are My Beloved Son in whom I am well pleased." And the Holy Spirit of God came down and settled upon Him in physical form like a dove. And there they all were again at last, all three: family, intimacy, union, One.

It was in that glorious state that the Holy Spirit led Jesus out into the wilderness "to be tempted by the devil."[10] What? Whatever happened to "Lead us not into temptation?"[11] Did God drive Jesus into the wilderness to try and to test Him, to see if He would stand and not buckle under? Was God putting Him through the fire to see if He could follow through and be the Messiah? Did God use the devil as His purging tool, His Divine pruning shears? Is the devil the agent for our purging and purification? Wait. What is it that makes us pure?

I'd like to suggest that, rather than God leading Jesus into the desert to be snared by the devil, God led Jesus into the wilderness to lead the devil into His trap, which is Jesus: man who is one with God and secure in His identity as a Son, filled with His Spirit, aligned with the plumb line of Heaven, overflowing with God's pleasure. God always works *from* victory and not *for* victory. Jesus didn't struggle under temptation to win a victory; He was the Victorious One displayed before powers and principalities and shining forth the victory we all always have in God, who always leads us in triumph in Christ, and through us, manifests the sweet aroma of the knowledge of God everywhere we go.[12]

In the same way, God enticed Pharaoh and his army to follow after Israel—not to trap Israel between the warriors and the sea, as it appeared to some, but to lure that army into His trap, which is God in the midst of us, God among His People, a pillar of fire and a mighty wind that parted the sea. The word of God was spoken forth, and the rod of our authority in God stretched out, and the very elements obeyed. When He brings us face-to-face with the enemy, it is an opportunity for us to choose where we will look, what we will focus upon. When our eyes are fixed on Him, He always proves Himself and "only does wondrous things."[13] If fixed on the enemy, we invite intimidation, fear, discouragement, and hopelessness. We magnify what we focus upon. When we magnify the Lord, He becomes larger than anything and everything, in our own minds at last, and then He proves His Good and pleasing and perfect will[14] in us and through us. Then the enemy that confronts us dwindles in magnitude, and we hear God say as He did to Israel: "Do not be afraid. Stand still, and see the salvation of the LORD, which He will accomplish for you today. For [this enemy] whom you see today, you shall see again no more, forever. The LORD will fight for you and you shall hold your peace."[15] We get to keep our peace, remain in peace, and watch God perform His victory before our eyes, while He makes us look like "more than conquerors."[16]

God's will is to put on display His manifold wisdom in us, *Christ in us, the hope of glory.*[17] He does it again and again. And so He took Israel to the borders of His Promised Land and told them

He brought them out of slavery that He might bring them in, to give them the land He promised.[18] He sent the spies in to see what He offered, and they saw that it was good and fruitful. Two of them were thrilled, and ten of them magnified the enemy, the problem, the giants—and those ten became "like grasshoppers in our own sight."[19] Two men looked at God in the midst of them and declared the land was theirs. Six hundred thousand warriors who met God in the wilderness forgot that God had brought them face-to-face with the enemy to display God's victory, to shine forth with the brilliance of a people with the Living God in the midst of them, *the manifold wisdom of God displayed before powers and principalities.*[20] Those six hundred thousand chose to stay in the wilderness for forty years and die there, never entering into all His promises. And we have identified the Wilderness Experience with their failure instead of with God's victories. Joshua, Caleb, David, John the Baptist, and Paul are all examples of the ones who met God in the wilderness and were forever changed so that when they met the enemy there, that enemy had nothing in them.[21] They simply weren't impressed.

Will you come away into the wilderness for a life-changing encounter with God? Will you let Him love you, fill you, transform you, and then let Him lure the enemy into His trap, which is you in Him and Him in you? It's pretty overwhelming: first you're over-whelmed with Him in you, and then the glimpse you get of the enemy just before you hide yourself in God can be a little over-whelming. Simply don't forget the focus … He has prepared a table for you right in the presence of your enemies.[22] He wants to honor you, to feast and nourish you, to serve you right there where the enemy has to watch how much the Living God loves you.

And then after that glorious proof of His good and pleasing and perfect will in you, you get to return, as Jesus did, "in the power of the Spirit … and news of Him went out through all the surrounding region."[23]

THE WILD PLACES OF GOD

It was in the wild places of my life
that I met HIM.
I was living in the mountains,
sleeping under the stars,
hiking the peaks,
drinking from the streams,
and experiencing the raw power
and beauty of the creation.
I asked if I could meet
the Maker of it all,
the Designer,
the Creator.
and HE came to me
and introduced HIMSELF to me,
and I fell under the wild ecstasy
of HIS love
and have never been the same.
I met with the Author of Life
and I came ALIVE!

CHAPTER 4

KINGDOM OF ABUNDANCE

"Our Father, dwelling in the Heavenly Realms,
may the glory of Your Name be the center on which our lives turn.
Manifest Your Kingdom realm,
and cause every purpose to be fulfilled on earth,
just as it is fulfilled in Heaven."

—JESUS[1]

I love to meditate on His Kingdom alive inside of me. Jesus said the Kingdom isn't over here or over there, and it doesn't come by observation, but the Kingdom of Heaven is within us.[2] That realm where the King rules and has dominion and exercises His authority and power is right inside us where the Holy Spirit has taken up residence. Holy Spirit has several roles on the inside. One is to lead us into All Truth.[3] Another is to take what belongs to Jesus and manifest it to us, declare it and make it known to us—everything that is Jesus's![4] Holy Spirit is the holiness of God inside us and washes us with renewing and regeneration,[5] transforming us from glory to glory as we look into Jesus.[6] He will bear witness with our spirits that we are sons and daughters, connected to the Father.[7] He'll give Life to our physical bodies as He lives in us.[8] We are His temple, the Holy of Holies where the very Presence of God dwells.[9] We as an entire body of believers are called "the fullness of Him who fills all in all,"[10] and we have become as living stones, built together into a holy habitation of God by His Spirit.[11] We're the manifold wisdom of God displayed before powers and principalities.[12]

How did we ever come into such a favored position? Grace! It's nothing we have done or could ever do.

> "He has delivered us from the power of darkness and conveyed us into the Kingdom of the Son of His love."
>
> —PAUL[13]

Let me ask you, concerning that verse in Colossians: How much work did we do in that sentence? Nothing! He has done it all and then freely given it to us—everything His beloved Son deserves, and all of His Kingdom and His inheritance we receive as a free gift. This is Grace!

As I was reading that verse one day, I sensed Holy Spirit ask me, "What were you delivered from, and what were you transported into?" I reread the words and thought about it. I was delivered from a power, the power of darkness. But I was transported into a Kingdom, the Kingdom of the Son whom He loves! Note that a power and a Kingdom are not the same. A power is simply strength, might, or force, and in this case, one that sought to keep us in darkness. It's the realm where there is only darkness. Darkness is not a generative energy but simply the absence of light. This power is keeping us blinded to the light.

> "... the god of this world has blinded the minds of the unbelieving so that they might not see the light of the

gospel of the glory of Christ, who is the image of God …
For God, who said, 'Light shall shine out of darkness,' is
the One who has shone in our hearts to give the light of the
knowledge of the glory of God in the face of Christ."

—PAUL[14]

How does he blind the minds? Since darkness is not a creative
energy or force in itself, but rather the absence of a creative energy
or force, the power of darkness is in the lies we believe. When our
minds are under the influence of lies and our hearts are unbeliev-
ing of Truth, we partner with those lies through agreement, and
they become the power that keeps us from experiencing the light
and knowing all its benefits. We come under the mindset of this
world, whose god is "a liar and the father of lies," says Jesus.[15] And
then we are completely in the dark as to this absolutely phenomenal
Kingdom of light and love and abundance that is all around us.
We simply do not see it. Then we lead with our blinded minds, our
intellects try to figure Truth out, and I hear people say, "I'm getting
it into my mind, but I'm trying to get it from there down into
my heart." It will never happen! You are going the wrong direction.
Truth shines into our hearts, and the overflow then brings enlight-
enment to our minds![16] We believe with our hearts![17]

But God delivered us from that power of darkness; He drew
us out to Himself; He placed us not only in the Kingdom of the
Son He loves, but even placed us into Christ, and then He placed
Christ in us![18] God has set us up, and we are free from the power
of that blindness, free to experience the fullness and brilliant light
of the Kingdom of the Son of His love since we are now in Him,
in the Son He loves![19]

A Kingdom is much greater than a power. While a power may
have a hierarchy of influence or control, a true Kingdom implies
righteous government and an orderly system with safety, order for
the welfare, prosperity, and fruitfulness of its citizens; it has

protection, justice, and benefits to promote a thriving economy. And a Kingdom takes its character from the character of its King. This King is Wonderful Counselor, Mighty God, Everlasting Father, Prince of Peace, and of the increase of His government and peace there will be no end.[20] He's a good, good King!

Under the mindset of this world, under the power of darkness, the lies that control us are those specifically of lack and limitation. It's all we cannot be, don't have, the not enoughs: not enough money, water, natural resources, talent, strength, good looks, intelligence, love, acceptance, friends, not good enough, fast enough, wealthy enough, smart enough, and especially not enough anointing. And the list goes on.

John tells us in his first letter to believers that "the whole world lies in wickedness."[21] This word for "wickedness" is not merely moral impurity, though it includes it. It means "malignant, toilsome, painful, full of labors and annoyances, hardships, pressed and harassed by labors, full of striving and performance."[22] There is always a pressing, a constraint, a narrowing of options, a limitation of possibility that causes us to struggle and strive to work our way into increase. This is the mindset that covers the world and keeps people from seeing there is a Kingdom of Abundance that supersedes this physical realm. Where the thief has come to steal, kill, and destroy, to narrow our options and squeeze us, rob us of hope and joy, and limit what's possible, Jesus has come in the opposite spirit to give us Life and Life More Abundantly![23] There's always a lie present to get us to work for what already has been freely given.

"In the world you will have tribulation, but take courage; I have overcome the world."

—JESUS[24]

The very word used here for "tribulation" means "to be pressed, crushed, squeezed like grapes in a wine press." The mindset of the world under its lies of lack and limitation are working to press and squeeze out the joy and glorious freedom we have in Christ. But when we know who we are in Him and that it was for freedom that He made us free, as we are pressed and squeezed by this world's circumstances, all that comes out is the wine of righteousness, peace, and joy in the Holy Spirit![25] The most commonly used Greek word for salvation means "saved, healed, delivered, made whole, open, wide and free."[26] We have been brought into the glorious freedom of the children of God, and no one can snatch us out of His hands.[27]

IT STARTED IN THE GARDEN

God's good and pleasing and perfect will for us has always been abundance. He created the earth to be fruitful and good, each part designed to reproduce abundantly.[28] Then He set man and woman in a garden in the midst of the earth and told them to be fruitful and multiply and from that garden incubator, to fill the whole earth. In the midst of the garden was the Tree of Life, from which they could eat freely and live forever. They were commissioned with a wonderful job, along with the fruitful multiplication job, and that was to nurture and protect the garden[29] as they expanded their stewardship over it into the whole world—a king and queen learning stewardship as they became servant guardians and overseers of a planet of abundance.

It looked like the role Lucifer longed for, but he missed the stewardship part; he only saw the ruler/overseer/king—"worship me"—part of the equation. And that has been the challenge to every leader ever since: to be boss or servant. It must have infuriated him to see man and woman given this as a free offer, a grace and favor unearned and undeserved. And here God placed man right in front of him, on the earth Lucifer had fallen onto like lightning from Heaven,[30] bound there with his cohorts in chains of darkness.[31] God prepared a table for man in the presence of his enemies so all could see how much the everlasting God loves mankind![32]

So the opposition began. God had placed another tree in the garden, the Tree of the Knowledge of Good and Evil. A choice was given: one leads to life and the other to death. Remember, death is not a creative force; rather, it is the absence of life. But when one makes the choice for death, all manner of degeneration occurs that was not in the original design because the continuous surge of life flowing in and manifesting in abundance has been cut off.

"… I have set before you life and death, blessing and the curse. So choose life in order that you may live …"

—GOD[33]

There was, of course, a deception, a lie man had to agree with before he could fall into darkness. There's always a lie to get us to work for what has already been freely given. They partnered with the lie of not enough—that, if they would do something, they would "be like God …" They were in fact created in His image and likeness already.[34] So they chose to know good and evil instead of knowing God, light and dark instead of glorious light in whom there is no shadow of darkness. They chose life and death instead of abundant and eternal life. They chose duality instead of oneness. And in that choice, man became the judge, with an ever-shifting standard, of what is "good and evil." Truth became relative instead of a person.[35] Through that choice, man turned over his inheritance of a garden, a kingdom, and a planet to the deceiver. And the great cracking, grinding rift began like an earthquake, tearing apart the very fabric of creation.

In giving man that choice, God risked all for the purpose of love. Connecting with God is experiencing love, and the knowledge of God is everlasting life![36] In His great love for us, He gave us life and abundance, all wrapped up in truth and the experience of oneness. The deceiver offered a world of duality: good and evil, light and darkness, abundance and lack, truth and lies, and in that duality, we are deceived into believing that it's normal and OK to have a little bit of truth in the lie, or a little lie in the truth; we can have some light in the darkness and some darkness in the light, some good in the evil and some evil in the good. It is, after all, the knowledge of good and evil.

But the Designer, the Imaginer of it all, the Lord of the inheritance, had another idea. Mankind was to be heir of all the promises and the Kingdom. And so He came, born as a man, born of a virgin, entering as a fragile baby into His own creation so that He as a man could regain the inheritance and the Kingdom He had purposed to give to man. He was not caught off guard as He took that daring risk to give man choice. He already had a plan. He was the Lamb slain from the foundation of the world![37]

Because the thief came only to steal, kill, and destroy, Jesus then came in power and authority to destroy the works of the enemy[38] so we may have that Life and Life more abundantly which He had originally given and always planned for us. Plan A all the time! As we see those two job descriptions functioning all around us, please remember who is the author of each one and do not confuse the two! Steal, kill, destroy—the enemy; Life and Life more abundantly—Jesus.[39]

THE ABUNDANT MINDSET

For twenty years, Linda and I led teams into huge New Age gatherings where we would camp for two weeks in a national forest somewhere in the US with the goal and commission to be the Body of Christ in the midst of twenty thousand countercultural revelers, shamans, pagans, and searchers. Our goals were simple: to love and worship God and be loved by Him, to fall in love with each other on our team, and to let that love overflow into the vast array of people drawn to us by that love and brilliant light while we served them from a place of love-fueled Abundance. We would haul all our camping and cooking equipment plus food supplies on gurneys and by backpack for a mile or more into the forest, often blazing a new trail over uncharted territory through the trees and over streams and rocks and up and down many hills. Over the course of the years, we grew into a village of 150.

The supplies were always limited by what we could carry and the meals by how much we could prepare for a given event. Hours were spent in joy-filled camaraderie around the kitchen chopping table as feasts were prepared with love in The Bread of Life Kitchen. We wanted to display the excellence of His Kingdom in everything from the construction of our camp to hygiene and cleanliness to our wash stations and latrines and to the quality of the meals we prepared. We planned our meals for about four hundred people, based on our food supplies and twenty-gallon cooking pots. But because we delighted in such gourmet fare as elk steak fajitas, wild boar with honey-mustard sauce, Mediterranean tabbouleh, salmon pasta salad, and sweet and sour duck on a bed of rice, the attendance consistently was closer to 1,000 hungry campers. And every day, as the queue grew longer and the numbers increased and the spoon began to scrape the bottom of the pot, we'd look into the abundance of Heaven and resist the temptation to give smaller portions to stretch it out, but instead rise up with joy, knowing that our God is a God of abundance. Then we would scoop out huge helpings, scraping the bottom of the pot each time as we'd look into the eyes of the campers, smile, and fill their bowls. Sometimes, I would place the lid partially over the pot so I wouldn't look into the limitation in the bottom but continue to celebrate and give thanks for the abundance of Heaven. Our team became used to the regular litany: "Thank You God, and *multiply it*!"

We'd often feed for hours, scooping out abundance whilst scraping the pot with each flourish until everyone was fed, and then we'd lift the lid to see a truly empty pot. *How do You* do *that, Lord? You consistently amaze us with Your goodness!*

CHAPTER 5

FROM HAVING ACCESS TO TAKING POSSESSION

*"And He brought us out from there, that He might bring us in
to give us the land which He swore to give our fathers."*
—MOSES[1]

How many men are six hundred thousand? Take a Bible, put your finger between the books of Malachi and Matthew, and begin to flip the pages from Genesis through Malachi. Watch all those words flip past. There are approximately six hundred thousand words in the Old Testament. Every word is a man who was twenty years or older when Israel was delivered from Egypt and brought to the border of the Promised Land. Every one of them died in the wilderness.[2] Though God brought them out of slavery, they wouldn't let go of the slave inside, the victimization, the poverty mindset, the orphan within.

We were all slaves and victims—but Jesus came and took all our sin, guilt, shame, and every curse upon Himself, becoming the ultimate victim on our behalf, setting us free at the cross so that now every victim has the opportunity to become a new creation in the Presence of the Living God in order that we might enter into all the promises of God. It isn't a function of our great strength, our righteousness, or even our own faith, whether great or small. All it takes is recognizing what He has done for us and then agreeing with what He promises He will do. Paul uses the accounting term "reckon" or "count."[3] It's a simple addition of the things God says are true and reckoning them placed in our account while He takes all our deficit upon Himself. The faith to believe it is a gift from Him! He says so in Romans 10: "Faith comes by hearing, and hearing by the word of God."[4]

The very ability to hear is inspired by God's voice; when God speaks, he who has ears to hear let him hear …[5] And when our ears respond to His truth, faith comes! God has made it simple and straightforward while also leaving in the choice clause. Yes, we can choose to argue, disagree, look with skepticism upon a phenomenal offer that is "really too good to be true," or we can meditate on what He has done, what He says is true, and what He says He will do. Choices.

The apostle Paul warned the believers not to make things too complicated:

> "I fear, lest somehow, as the serpent deceived Eve by His craftiness, so your minds may be corrupted from the simplicity that is in Christ."
>
> —PAUL[6]

The six hundred thousand couldn't enter into His rest, His promises, or His purposes because of their unbelief.[7] So God raised up a new generation, born in freedom, raised on promise, trained in miracles and displays of His power, anticipating their destiny. He brought this generation to the Jordan River that they might cross over into the Land of All His Promises. And He provided a new leader to bring them across.

While Moses brought them out—his name means "to draw out"—Joshua was the one appointed to bring them in. His name means "the Lord is Salvation." After the end of six hundred thousand words of history, poetry, prophecy, and promise, Jesus—the Greek form of the name Joshua—leads us into a New Covenant, a Better Covenant,[8] with the opening of the gospels and the introduction into the plan of the ages. I'm paraphrasing here what Paul said in 2 Corinthians 1:20 to the church:

In Him (Jesus) all the Promises of God are "yes," and we in Him say "amen" to that yes, agreeing with His fulfillment of the Promises, and this way God is glorified.

We have a powerful prophetic picture in the book of Joshua for our entry into the Land of All His Promises. Three times in the first chapter, God says: "Be strong and courageous!"[9] God must have felt Joshua needed that strength and courage. Then He proceeds to make a series of outrageous promises:

Now therefore, arise, go over this Jordan, you and all this people, to the land which I am giving to them—the children of Israel. Every place that the sole of your foot will tread upon I have given you, as I said to Moses. From the wilderness and this Lebanon as far as the great river, the River Euphrates, all the land of the Hittites, and to the Great Sea toward the going down of the sun, shall be your territory. No man shall be able to stand before you all the days of your life; as I was with Moses, so I will be with you. I will not leave you nor forsake you. Be strong and of good courage, for to this people you shall divide as an inheritance the land which I swore to their fathers to give them. Only be strong and very courageous, that you may observe to do according to all the law which Moses My servant commanded you; do not turn from it to the right hand or to the left, that you may prosper wherever you go.[10]

Who crossed over into all the outlandish promises of God? We see that first it was a Freeborn People, a people who either were not of warrior age when they left slavery or who were born in freedom during the forty years in the wilderness. Next we see that it was the priests who bore "the Ark of the Presence of God in the midst of the people" who were the first to step into the river, which was at spring flood stage. And finally, it was these priests who carried the Presence of the Living God. All Israel was called to sanctify themselves, set themselves apart, "For tomorrow the LORD will do wonders among you."[11] They were told that when they saw the priests bearing the Ark of the Covenant of the Lord our God, they were to go after it. Yet they had to maintain a distance so they could see the way to go, for they had never gone that way before.

We are now a Freeborn People: the Son has set us free, and we are free indeed![12] It was for freedom that Christ set us free;[13] the Truth has set us free.[14] We are a now a free people, born-again into the glorious liberty of the children of God.

We are a Priestly People: In 1 Peter 2, we read that we "are a royal priesthood," we "are a chosen generation, a royal priesthood, a holy nation, His own special people …"[15] Revelation 1:6 tells us Jesus "has made us kings and priests to His God and Father …"[16] A priest is one who ministers to God on behalf of the people, and we who are now in Him, one with Jesus our great High Priest, stand before God on behalf of the whole world—interceding on their behalf and bringing our worship of Him on the earth before all men.

We carry the very Presence of God: we are temples of God and the Spirit of God dwells in us.[17] And our bodies are the temple of the Holy Spirit, who is in us, whom we have from God,[18] in whom we also are being built together into a holy habitation of God through the Spirit.[19] We have become that Ark, that Holy of Holies on the earth where the concentrated glory of the presence of God lives and shines forth from above the "Mercy Seat."

We are now those people the Lord is taking where we've never been before; we're the ones He has invited into All of His Promises. We have full access to them all, just as Israel did from the day they left Egypt. They didn't earn the promises, they came as a gift. We too must receive our inheritance as a gift and a promise. But they wouldn't agree with God, so He raised up the next generation.

What happened when that new generation stepped into the floodwaters that separated them from walking in and possessing the promises? Joshua 3 tells us that when the feet of the Free-born Priests who bore the Presence of God stepped into the down-flowing of the Jordan River, the flood that poured down into the Dead Sea was cut off and piled upstream in a heap.[20] Can you visualize it? The river keeps flowing from the mountains upstream, yet it stops at a certain point and begins to pile up in a great heap of water, ever growing in height as the flow keeps coming. For hours! It continued to flow and pile up until the river bed was dry, and close to three million people crossed over. Astounding!

And where was this point where the flood piled up into a heap? It was at a city called Adam. Nowhere else in the Bible is this city called Adam mentioned. I believe it is a prophetic picture. When a Freeborn, Priestly People who carry the very Presence of God approach the Land of All God's Promises, the down-flow of humanity that pours from Adam into—what was the name of that sea? Oh yes, the *Dead* Sea—is cut off. All the reproach, sin, carnality, and failure of man from the time of Adam was constantly flowing as a muddy river at flood time, overflowing its banks, flowing downward into death, the Dead Sea from which nothing flows out. And then came Jesus, our Joshua. He stepped into the Jordan to be baptized as a man, a freeborn man, our great High Priest, one who was filled with the Holy Spirit, who carried the very Presence of God. And all that down-flow of humanity that flowed into death was cut off and piled up in one heap, a great distance away at Adam, the city that is beside Zaretan.[21] *Zaretan* means "pierced." This great flood of guilt and sin and shame that flowed from Adam was cut off and piled back to the Second Adam, the One who stood in the place of the first Adam and the One who was pierced for all mankind's transgression and iniquity. And we who have been set free, made free men and priests unto our God and King and filled with His Spirit so that we carry the very Presence of God in human tents—we get to go freely into all of His promises!

What Paul wrote in 2 Corinthians 1:20 is so on point that I have to paraphrase it yet again:

"All the promises of God are 'Yes!' in Jesus, and we who are in Christ declare 'Amen!' to the glory of God."

Jesus has made the way. He *is* the way, as well as the truth and the life. We are complete in Him, and God's plan for mankind is fulfilled by us in Him, a holy, set-free, priestly people filled with His Spirit, entering into all of His promises, taking back territory the enemy has inhabited, liberating the land from the curse and bondage and bringing all creation into the glorious freedom of the children of God.

"The created world itself can hardly wait for what's
     coming next.
Everything in creation is being more or less held back.
God reins it in until both creation and all the creatures
     are ready
and can be released at the same moment into the glorious
     times ahead.

Meanwhile, the joyful anticipation deepens.
All around us we observe a pregnant creation.
The difficult times of pain throughout the world are
　　simply birth pangs.
But it's not only around us; it's within us.
The Spirit of God is arousing us within.
　We're also feeling the birth pangs.
These sterile and barren bodies of ours are yearning for
　　full deliverance.
That is why waiting does not diminish us,
any more than waiting diminishes a pregnant mother.
We are enlarged in the waiting. We, of course, don't see
　　what is enlarging us.
But the longer we wait, the larger we become,
and the more joyful our expectancy."

—PAUL[22]

CHAPTER 6

THE RIVER
OF GOD IS FULL
OF WATER

"Then the angel showed me the river of the water of Life, as clear as crystal,
flowing from the throne of God and of the Lamb."
—JOHN THE REVELATOR[1]

EAST AFRICA 1994–1995

My first month in Africa is still a kaleidoscope of images: war was just over but near enough to touch in Rwanda; we could hear the thunder of bombs as we waited at the airport with two of our children in Bujumbura, Burundi, and some of the roads in Uganda were an obstacle course of blown-out craters while stuccoed walls were pockmarked with bullet scars. Yet for all the devastation, the land itself was paradise. Banana trees showed off their huge blossoms even as they hung heavy with the ripening clusters of their twenty-eight varieties. Bougainvillea was a blaze of color everywhere, coffee trees in full bloom perfumed the night air, and the jungle was an outrage of tropical fruit of every kind.

But it was the people we fell in love with. We worked our way through the crowded kiosks and sellers forming a native market that hugged the lakeshore and spilled over into many boats of varied sizes moored in the shallow water at the edge of Lake Victoria. In perfect African timing, a longboat eventually arrived to carry us and our stuff across the lake. While locals waded through the knee-deep water to climb aboard, they insisted the white "Mazungus" be carried to the boat. (Slightly embarrassing for us.) The long, narrow boat was packed with joy-filled, black-skinned Ugandans and ten of us from the US looking very, very white. As we made friends with the others in the open longboat, the woman sitting by me dipped a faded red plastic cup into the lake and had a cool drink. Our team glanced at each other in surprise, as we had been cautioned not to even swim in the lake because of the parasites. To her, it was simply water.

Three hours after our scheduled arrival time, we pulled into a grassy cove and saw on the hilltop dozens of people sitting and watching for us. They all rose up and, clapping joyfully, sang us ashore and up the hill and then all the way into the village, chanting Lugandan songs of welcome. They had been waiting for us the whole time with no sign of offense at our tardiness, only happy to greet us with songs and open hearts. Men piled our backpacks onto bicycles and walked them alongside us down the dusty road, passing through banana groves on our way to the compound of family huts in the jungle village where we would be staying.

Everywhere we went, the predominant and impacting sight was the beautiful African women in extravagantly patterned, boldly colored fabric bearing twenty-liter jugs on their heads, filling the roads as they walked up to four kilometers each day to get water for their families. When I walked with them, I discovered that the water source often bore no resemblance to "clean and pure." The sight marked me, and my wife Linda and I came home with the desire to bring clean water into villages. It took fourteen years to see that dream come to pass.

I returned in the spring of 2007 to explore the possibility of drilling wells in five villages in Kenya and Uganda. The more I traveled, the more I was overwhelmed by the great black hole of need. It seemed every village in East Africa was lacking clean water. Then God spoke to me in His sure, calm voice and told me not to be overwhelmed by the magnitude of the need but to look only at what was immediately before me. We could take on one thing at a time and be the answer to that single need. We raised finances in the States and were able to provide clean water to one region that had an orphanage, a school, and several villages. That in itself was rewarding, but I learned something else.

I learned there are underground aquifers beneath every area of the globe. Where the land may be dying, if you drill deep enough, you can find rivers flowing even under the desert. These rivers are invisible to man, and the earth and her people suffer without their gift. "The River of God is full of water," declares David the prophet-king.[2] All the riches of Heaven flow into the created realms in this River of God, described to us in His Word and revealed to us by His Spirit. But it is all so invisible to us as we struggle in a world that lack and limitation has defined until our agreements with them have made it our experience and reality. Yet the River of God is *full of water.* How do we access it? How do we partake of it and possess it? And how do we share it, releasing it for the benefit of others?

That's what my life is about.

PRIMING THE PUMP

When we lived on a farm in the mountains of Colorado, we had a well. It was hand-dug, only about thirty feet deep, as the water table there is high. The walls had been rocked up, and should you ever want to, you could climb down into it. But I assure you, you would never want to. There were snakes down there, and occasionally a mouse would fall in, and his floating body would dissolve into a substance we called "jelly mouse."

We never drank the water; we only used it for washing and irrigating gardens and lawns, as it was full of alkali and minerals. There was an electric pump in the well house that worked most of the time. At one point, however, the foot valve went out. This meant that when you pumped water into the lines to the gardens, you could have a great flow, but when you stopped pumping, all the water in the lines drained back into the well as the foot valve never shut to hold the water, leaving all the pipes dry and full of only air. If you tried to turn the pump on, it would attempt to pump the air but never catch any water, which risked burning the pump out. Before we pulled up the thirty feet of pipe to replace the foot valve, we used to do a thing called "priming the pump."

We kept a five-gallon bucket full of water in the pump house at all times. When you wanted to irrigate or wash, you had to pour the water from the bucket down the pipe and into the pump, and when the line filled, you'd quickly hit the switch and the pump motor would whirr and then catch and pump the water, creating a flow. As long as it was flowing, you didn't have to be concerned with the foot valve, as it was always open.

We are like deep wells drilled into the River of God. All around us is a barren landscape dying for lack of Living Water. But the River of God is *full* of water! And we are His pipelines created to water the dry and thirsty land around us. When our lines become drained and dry, the metaphor "full of hot air" becomes a reality. Then it's all only a concept, words without substance or power, and we must return to ministering in the Holy Spirit and Power.[3] For that to happen, we must prime our pumps to get back to the substance of Heaven that the earth is hungering and thirsting for. Just like on our farm, we must take that which came from the well and pour it back into the lines before we can pump truth and not burn out. We drew up from the River of God truth from His word, hope from His promises, prophecies that came from His mind and heart. We need to refresh ourselves with these, pouring into us His truths,

His words, His promises, and the prophecies He's declared over us of future and promise. He's given us the gifts of His Spirit, and we need to reactivate these. All of these are in the buckets that stand by the pump, waiting to be used, embraced, indulged in, recognized, and delighted in should we ever become weary or dry. As we drink deeply from them our dryness ends, the thrill of our new creation identity re-emerges, and *life* displaces emptiness as He comes with "the washing of regeneration and renewing of the Holy Spirit, whom He poured out on us abundantly through Jesus Christ our Savior."[4] We have the choice to stay always aware of our connection as deep wells drilled into the River of God, always having access and drawing from its abundance. But if we believe any lies of separation or disconnect and resort to performance and our own efforts to do the work of the ministry, we will become dryer and dryer. When our outer platform becomes larger than our inner world, then that outer platform will cause a crumbling of the dry and substance-less dogma we are trying to promote, for the Gospel is not an issue of words but of the Holy Spirit and power![5] We must keep our awareness of that inner connection tapped into His limitless, eternal River and let our ever-growing stewardship of His gifts and promises increase so we can continue to see the world around us changed by His power and love.

ARTESIAN WELLS

When we lived in the San Luis Valley of Colorado, we experienced another sort of well. The valley was surrounded by high mountains: on the east by the Sangre de Cristo Range (which means "Blood of Christ") and on the west by the Continental Divide. The mountain springs and runoff created pressure in the underground aquifers beneath the valley floor. Many of these wells drilled into high-pressure systems that sent the water up with such force that the wells had to be capped and then piped to divert the water where it was needed. These artesian wells had no pumps but operated under the gushing power of the underground water's pressure.

There are times when we, under the strength of the Holy Spirit gushing through our inner man, operate with such power we have to learn ways to direct this surge of heavenly energy. In those times, it seems like miracles happen everywhere we are because those miracles are the love language of Heaven. Sometimes, the huge power surges that come from the Holy Spirit moving mightily are such that our physical bodies react with unexplainable manifestations. It can become difficult to walk, even impossible to move at times. We may reel about as drunken men, twitch and jerk, or laugh and cry uncontrollably when the moving of the Holy Spirit is so strong. Though it can be confusing and defies our ability to understand it, the results of letting the Spirit surge and then beginning to love and enjoy what is beyond our control allows us to become intimate with a power that is way beyond our own and connects us with an appreciation of the One who came to live inside. It's humbling and even frightening at times, but He flushes clean the ones He flows through, and the transformation is worth way more than all the discomfort. Ezekiel, Daniel, and John the Beloved are among those who experienced the powerful surge of presence and ended face-down on the ground ...[6] in fear and trembling and "like a dead man."[7] If you are overwhelmed by the outpourings of His Spirit, you're in good company!

BLUE SKY AT THE BEACH

I was speaking at a conference in Melbourne, Australia, that lasted a week—morning, afternoon, and evening. It was quite a full schedule, and a beloved friend of mine asked if he could give me a short holiday. He lived on the island of Tasmania where there are unspoiled, pristine beaches down the east coast. His request was to fly me over and drive me down the coast to spend a blue-sky day at the beach. What is the correct response to such an invitation?

"Yes, please!"

I arrived Friday evening, and we hiked up to some waterfalls and enjoyed his wife's outstanding hospitality. The next morning, we awoke for the adventure—only to see stormy dark skies and pouring-down rain. The weather report said there'd be thunderstorms all day. Being of similar disposition, we looked at each other with a sparkle in our eyes and said: "Blue sky at the beach!" We hopped in his car and took off in a torrent of rain for the two-hour drive to the first beach, declaring with joy: "Thank You, God, for the blue sky at the beach!" Halfway there, we drove over a mountain pass, and the storm grew worse. It started hailing, but our joy only increased. It was still raining when we arrived at the bluffs overlooking the bay, as we viewed the expanse of sandy beach and the pounding surf under an ominous sky of dark grey storm clouds. We ran down onto the beach and along the edge of the water declaring: "Thank You, God, for the blue sky at the beach!"

Why could we delight in this moment and thank God for a blue sky we didn't see? Because we knew that behind those storm clouds, no matter how distant, there was, in fact, a blue sky and that the sun was shining. We chose to identify with that reality rather than the dark-cloud reality and in so doing, to call the blue-sky reality in. We spoke to the clouds and commanded them to part and called out to the sunshine, welcoming it to break through the clouds and shine on us. We spoke to the greater reality that was presently invisible to us—there was actually more clear sky between us and the sun than there were clouds between us—and we called it into our experience.

This may sound like a ridiculous pipe dream or wishful thinking, but it is actually the perfect illustration of faith in the heavenly realm breaking through into our circumstances to bring every sort of miracle. In life, there are the storm clouds of sickness, loss of a job, poverty, relational dysfunction, hopelessness, and death. But in a realm we cannot see—a realm that is infinite and much, much greater than our visible condition—we have clarity and the answers to all our needs. We have an Open Heaven.[8] This is why God's word admonishes us:

> "... we do not look at the things which are seen, but at the things which are not seen. For the things which are seen are temporary [passing away], but the things which are not seen are eternal."
>
> —PAUL[9]

All of Heaven is invisible to us, but we have learned that it is a very real Kingdom and we have access to it—not by our own efforts or goodness, but by His Grace. Jesus became heir of all things for us[10] and has now made us co-heirs with Him of all things.[11] Our inheritance is preserved for us in Heaven where it is incorruptible, undefiled, and doesn't fade away.[12] It is kept safely in the bank of Heaven where it cannot be stolen or depleted. The Holy Spirit in us is the deposit that guarantees that inheritance.[13] He takes what belongs to Jesus and manifests it to us.[14] He is our ability to do the works Jesus did—and even greater works, now that Jesus is with the Father and They have sent the promise of the Father, the gift of the Holy Spirit, to be in us and upon us.[15] God is glorified when we take our ATM card to the bank in Heaven and withdraw some of our assets, blessing the Lord with all our soul and not forgetting all His benefits![16]

As we danced on the beach in the rain, celebrating God's goodness and calling forth the blue skies that lay hidden behind the stormy clouds, we spotted a tiny dot of blue in the midst of all those gray-black roiling clouds that filled the sky. Blue sky! We erupted with rejoicing and celebration, praise and thanksgiving. You would have thought the entire sky had turned bright summertime blue to hear us. Though it was only a spot the size of my thumb nail when I held up my hand, it was breakthrough.

One of the biggest keys to seeing increased breakthrough is to recognize when God is doing something and to connect with that. It's often easy to miss what He's doing when it starts out small, but when our eyes are looking for Him, we are attentive to every little change that occurs, and we recognize His hand in it. Every move He makes is Grace, and we connect with His Grace through our thanksgiving. He designed it that way in His infinite wisdom so that grace would not be an ethereal or intellectual concept but a dynamic, relational interaction wherein He supplies all the goods and we experience them as we first recognize them and then connect with them through thanksgiving and celebration. As our recognition spills over into thanksgiving, we find He has more planned for us, and thus we see increase. We don't manipulate God to do more through our thanksgiving; He has already planned more for us. The more we recognize and connect with what He is doing, the more we see Him do. It's a delightful win-win escalation.

As we celebrated the tiny spot of blue that peeked through the clouds, we began to see it grow larger, and within half an hour, the entire sky was gloriously blue! We spent the rest of that day on several beaches, rejoicing in the day He made just for us. At 5:00 p.m. we headed back to my friend's home where a fantastic meal and a meeting full of hungry people awaited us.

As soon as we hopped in the car, it poured down rain and continued to do so for the trip back. *You are so delightful and mischievous, God!*

We shared our adventure with the others, and one person said: "Don't you think it's a little presumptuous to think that God would change the weather just for you?"

I wanted to say, "Excuse me, I don't understand your question." Here's why: We're the sons that He loves! Presumption would set us against the heart of God, but we are only drawing closer to Him through this experience, for He resists the proud but gives grace to the humble.[17] It's never presumptuous for us to take Him at His word, to take His promises out for a test drive, to believe He gave us authority and dominion on this planet, to see that He calmed storms, or for us to want to do the things He did and even more ... the "greater works." Like the holy men and women of old in Hebrews 11:13, I can see the promises afar off, like when I am sick and need healing—and then I'm persuaded that they are for me, embrace them as my own, and declare that I am only a pilgrim and a stranger traveling through this experience of sickness. It is neither my home nor my identity; I am passing through it, and the faster the better.

We've changed the weather hundreds of times now and taught thousands of others to do it as well. There are times it has diverted disaster and times it has been for sheer joy. I've found God's delight in both of them. I've even been accused of having weather-changing angels who follow me as I've traveled to so many places where there have been storms and then it is beautiful while I am there. On our sailing adventures, so often squalls will dissipate in front of our eyes right before they reach us. I believe those weather angels might be real!

DEEP CRIES OUT TO DEEP

I feel the stirring, the deep, deep yearning
In my spirit, soul and body
Like when the earth cries out for rain.
I've felt often the fine slow rain,
The soft soaking rain
Fine as a mist
That gently nourishes the ground
And doesn't pelt the tender plants
But causes them to stretch upright and gladly greet the sky.
But I am yearning
For the pummeling rain,
The torrent that flattens my soul
Face down in the ground
All tears and snot and brokenness
Where I am wrapped up in the holy fear of God,
Where love and mercy collide
And intermix
With righteousness and truth,
Where there is only brilliant, all-consuming light
And there is no escape.

CHAPTER 7

INVASIONS OF JOY

*"These things I have spoken to you, that My joy may remain in you,
and that your joy may be full."*

—JESUS[1]

I can't remember a time since I first met Jesus that I have not experienced His joy. It's been a deep inner fountain that keeps bubbling up with unending, limitless, everlasting *life*. In the worst of all trials, He's been so close I've felt His arms wrap around me; I've sat on my bed, and He's held me when I've wept, while the wellspring of joy kept gushing.

There was a time in the past when I was surrounded by a number of very joy-less, unhappy Christians. One woman came by to tell me what was on her mind: "I think you're a phony," she declared.

"Oh, why is that?" I asked her.

"Because nobody is that happy all the time. I think you're faking it."

I pondered that statement and what it might look like to fake it, but I couldn't quite generate that image in my mind. I mean, you *can* actually have the real thing; it's free. She had decided I was in denial.

"Yeah, why are you so happy all the time?" asked a man who was her friend. It sounded like an accusation.

I had to think about it. *Why am I so happy all the time?*

"Lord, why am I so happy all the time?"

And then it hit me, wave after wave after wave of the captivating, personal, intimate revelation of His love for me. I was standing under an Open Heaven, affirmed by the Father as the son that He loves, aligned with the Plumb Line of God while past and future slipped out of focus and the clear resonance of the *now* of God washed over me. I was His pleasure and delight. It was fresh, spontaneous, unexpected, overwhelming, and delightful.

"Because He loves me," was all I could say.

"You act like you *believe* it," he replied emphatically, with a dubious stab.

That's my problem! It's true. I really believe it.

I've spent years exploring the reality of Him in me and I in Him. It's absolutely the most exciting adventure we can ever participate in. He lives in me. Really. The very idea wrecks me over and over again.

"You will show me the path of Life;
in Your presence is fullness of joy;
at Your right hand are pleasures forevermore."

—KING DAVID[2]

He's right here, in me, alive and speaking to me so I can experience His limitless, unending joy, and His joy in me fills me up to the brim with no empty spaces, until it overflows … in His presence. I was looking up the Hebrew word for "presence" so I could dive deeper into the experience of it. The word simply means "face." He's here, very close, and I am looking right into His face, His eyes, His glorious countenance. Paul, the follower of Jesus and anointed teacher, tells us in his letter to the Corinthians that "we all, with unveiled face, beholding as in a mirror the glory of the Lord, are being transformed into the same image from glory to glory, just as by the Spirit of the Lord."[3]

"I have told you these things so that My joy and delight may be in you, and that your joy may be made full and complete and overflowing."

—JESUS[4]

There are times when I'm walking about in awe of Him and overflowing joy just happens. They're like joy-releasing accidents. The first time I noticed such a thing affecting someone else in a public setting, I was in the crowded Healing Rooms at Bethel Church. I walked past a man and touched him on the shoulder. Physical touch is one of my love languages, and it was a simple greeting, a kind of blessing as I passed him. I'd never met the man before. As I continued walking, I heard a thud and turned to find him laid out on the ground laughing. Seemed like a good thing to me. Ten minutes later, I returned to the room, and he was still on the floor, rolling around, laughing uncontrollably. So I poked him a little with my finger, and he laughed harder. I went about my business and came back later to find him still on the floor, and the laughing had not diminished. I reached down to pick up his intake form to see why he had come into the Healing Rooms. Written on the line in block letters was the word: DEPRESSION. Yes! Depression, wiped out by an ambush of joy.

I was telling this story over the mic some months later to a large crowd of guests in our Healing Rooms. Each time we share a testimony of God's miraculous healing power, we find there is an impartation, a seed of faith to believe He'll do it again and an invitation to enter into that experience with Him for our own healing.[5] When it comes to healing, He's a repeat offender. He might just be a compulsive healer; He's so committed to healing He can't stop doing it. It's one of His names.[6]

There was a wave of fresh hope and joy that swept through the room as I shared the story. While I was speaking, my attention was drawn to a little two-year-old boy in front of me who began to walk around as if he were drunk, reeling and weaving, finally flopping over on his side on the floor and rolling around laughing. I thought he was mimicking what I was saying, and it was so ridiculously cute. About half an hour later, his mom came up to me, holding the boy in her arms. "He can't stop smiling!" she exclaimed to me.

"I know, I saw him earlier. I thought it was hysterical how he looked drunk and then fell down laughing."

"No, you don't understand," she said. "He's never laughed in his life. He's two years old, and he has never even smiled once in all his life, let alone laughed. Even when he was a baby, we could never get him to crack the tiniest smile. We've never seen anything but a sad face. Something left him, and he's completely changed!"

Wow! I was overwhelmed by the love of God and His tender kindness toward this family and this child who'd found a joy that shone into the deep, dark place of sadness and drove it out for the first time in his life! *Thank You, Jesus, You are so caring. You really do love to repeat the testimonies of Your goodness!* And the little boy smiled hugely and waved goodbye. Mom cried, and I was wrecked again.

> "You have enlarged the nation and increased their joy; they rejoice before you as people rejoice at the harvest, as war-riors rejoice when dividing the plunder. You have shattered the yoke that burdens them, the bar across their shoulders, the rod of their oppressor."
>
> —ISAIAH[7]

Sometime later, I was in a crowded house meeting in Australia. I placed my hand on a woman, and she dropped to the floor and laughed uncontrollably for a long time. I received a message from her several weeks later that she had been diagnosed with chronic depression, for which she had been on medication for five years. When she got up from her extended laughing stint, she realized she was thinking differently; she felt and saw things in a new way. She went to see her doctor, and he told her: "You're different. You are thinking differently, and your mind is responding in a new way." He decided to wean her off the meds, and she's been joy-filled since that time. *That's amazing how You changed it all in one encounter, God. Your joy flooded in and drove out five years of depression!*

> "[T]he former shall not be remembered or come to mind
> But be glad and rejoice forever in what I create …"
>
> —GOD[8]

I was meeting lots of new people in a very full house that overflowed with guests, and joy was pretty rampant there. As I put out my hand to introduce myself to a young woman seated on a couch, I noticed she would not look up into my face. So I held onto her hand to the point of awkwardness while she squirmed a little. Unwilling to let her hand go, I kept looking into her face, beaming brightly as she continued to avert her eyes. I had already introduced myself, so I thought no other words were needed. I kept pouring love into her through my hand; love streamed from my heart and the heart of Christ down my arm and into her. Several times, she tried to let go, but I wouldn't. There was nothing she could do to stop it from coming. She began to glance up briefly to see who this guy was, but she then quickly looked away. Her hand was stuck, and she didn't know what to do. She peeked again. I kept beaming, looking lovingly into her face. She bit her lip. Then she looked into my eyes for a brief moment. I saw years of terror and pain, gender confusion, victimization, terrible choices, shame, guilt, defenses, all in a flash, but I kept the love coming like a mighty river. She was locked in now, and a shadow passed across her face—and then the love broke through. Her countenance began to change before my eyes as peace and acceptance and the great, great love of God rushed into the void and filled it up. She smiled, then laughed. Her face radiated love and peace; she was the daughter God loved. It all happened without words, but there was a huge and immediate transformation. She glowed.

Later in the evening, after I had taught on healing, we had a time of activation where the people in the room prayed for one another and declared healing and saw conditions and symptoms leave and bodies get healed. It got really fun. I walked around coaching and encouraging men and women as they began to see God do miracles. As I walked up to the young woman who had been so dramatically changed, she was praying with a friend for an older woman who was deaf in her right ear. We tested it, and sure enough, she could hear nothing through that ear. I looked at the beautiful, transformed young woman and said, "The mute button is on." Without missing a beat, the young woman picked up an invisible remote control, pointed it at the older woman's ear, and pressed the "mute button." Instantly, the older woman's ear popped open, and the sound came on. She jerked and turned her head. We took her out of the noisy great room into a quiet hallway and stood her at one end facing the wall with her back to us. She covered her good left ear, and we slowly walked backward, farther and farther away from her, as we quietly spoke words and sentences and she repeated them. Finally, we asked her to turn around, and she was completely dumbfounded to see us all the way at the end of the hall as we quietly spoke and she was able to hear every word. Joy filled her as she realized God did that just for her!

It's amazing to me how we can see God do such wonders—and then hear complete lies about who we are.

It was springtime, a season I love for all the new life and hope that explodes in nature all around us. Yet somehow, I couldn't shake the lying feeling that my life wasn't important, didn't amount to anything, and I wasn't impacting the lives of others. I know it's a lie. I thought with joy about how much God loves me, and I knew that was the truth. I recalled stories of radical miracles that changed people forever. I laughed out loud at those thoughts and called them what they are: lies. But the feelings wouldn't go away; that strange sense of worthlessness persisted. I tried all the normal tricks, but it was tenacious. I could feel it in the core of my emotions.

The greatest temptation I could feel was to go around trying to get people to tell me I was important. I felt like I needed validation. I knew many people would be quick to affirm me, but my mind went to those who would be the most difficult to receive validation from, especially some authority figures in my life. It was stupid, but the feelings were persistent. They defied all logic, and they were messing with my thinking. So I talked to God about it.

I love You and what I get to do with You and what You do through me. Will You please encourage me that my life has value and impacts the lives of others? I won't ask anyone else right now; I just need to hear from You. Thanks. And I left it at that.

As He began to open my eyes, I saw that I was actually picking up a pervasive atmosphere that was affecting many people. It was like an outbreak of accusation, condemnation, that feeling of not being good enough that generated a desperate need for affirmation and validation. The "accuser of our brethren"[9] was releasing his slime just like the giant slurry bombers flying over the California wildfires drop a huge red liquid cloud of fire retardant that sticks to everything it falls upon. I began to take authority over it and focus on the atmosphere of Heaven, spreading around the "sweet aroma of the knowledge of Him ..."[10] and He began to invade my life with overwhelming encouragement. Every day for the next two weeks, I received an email, Facebook message, phone call, or personal contact from someone telling me some outstanding tale of a life forever changed.

"For the LORD takes pleasure in His people;
He will beautify the humble with salvation.
Let the saints be joyful in glory;
let them sing aloud on their beds."

—KING DAVID[11]

Right at that time, a twenty-year-old first-year student at Bethel School of Supernatural Ministry approached the front of the auditorium after a teaching session one night and asked if she could speak to me. There was that tentative air of an unknown student approaching a public figure that humbled me and made me smile. She said her mother told her if she ever got a chance to connect with me, she should tell me her story.

"Please do," I told her.

The mother had experienced a severe chemical imbalance all her life with bipolar surges that were so horrific she had been hospitalized at one point. The daughter said her mom had dealt with depression, panic, and torment as long as she could remember. This mother had come up to me at the end of a conference session several years before, asking for prayer. I looked into her intense and serious demeanor as she began to tell me a litany of problems, and I stopped her, placed my finger up to her lips, and said, "Shhh …" in a mischievous, playful way that offended her intellect. (She later told me she was so offended!) Then I placed my hands in the air above her head and wiggled my fingers, stating: "We're just going to rewire your brain." Bam! She went down. She told me she felt electricity rush through her brain, "re-wiring" it, and she knew she was different. She fell to the floor, laughing uncontrollably, overwhelmed by the Holy Spirit. I didn't really know the end of it all until her daughter told me the rest of the story. The mother was filled with joy; she began to think differently. She went off all her medications. The joy wouldn't quit.

The curious thing to me is that the attack I felt was aimed specifically at joy. I kept hearing derogatory accusations in my head that other people had powerful ministries and all I had was joy. I was just the goofy, happy guy—the village idiot. I was just a happy drunk, and that was slightly obnoxious. There was no real redemptive purpose, and I had nothing else to offer. I lacked credibility and scriptural accuracy. I really had nothing to offer except a laugh or two.

"God, your God, has anointed you,
pouring out the oil of joy on you
more than on anyone else."

—THE SONS OF KORAH[12]

The woman wrote to me, and later I met her in person. This is what she said: "I was drawn to your joy, and whenever I got into close proximity of you, the presence of the Lord was very strong on me like a heavy, heavy blanket. You prayed for a re-wiring of my brain, and you told me to keep my eyes on Jesus and hold onto the things He's told me and it will happen. I had no idea then the life-changing effect that prayer would have on me. From that moment forward, there has been a progressive sense of everything coming into divine order, both in my brain and in my life in general.

"One of my favorite words of all time is the word 'convergence': seemingly unrelated tributaries all coming together to form one mighty river. I have intense clarity in my thinking that is a miracle because, for quite some time now, I have struggled with my inability to focus. I also have an acute sense of 'knowing' so many things that I only had fragments and glimpses of before. The best part about it is that I know that I know that I know it isn't going to go away. God keeps reassuring me that it won't be like before. I won't lose it. He's not going anywhere. I get to walk in His peace now."

She told me three years later she was still 100 percent healed of chemical imbalance. Previously, her bipolar surges were almost always into the dark side, rarely ever on the manic upside. This had caused her circuits to short out, and she had ended up in a mental facility. She was on Lamyctal, a drug stronger than lithium, and when she returned from the conference to her doctor, he saw the change and worked with her to wean her off all medications in two weeks. All her friends have seen the remarkable transformation! After that, she went through a painful divorce after a twenty-eight-year marriage, and though it was extremely hard, she didn't sink back into the hopelessness and torment she used to live under. She was able to deal with difficulty.

> "But let all those rejoice who put their trust in You;
> let them ever shout for joy,
> because You defend them.
> Let those also who love Your Name be joyful in You."
> —KING DAVID[13]

There's something of a military stance we take when we choose joy. It establishes us in His strength; we find ourselves surrounded by His love like a fortress, and it seems a place of protection and immunity is reinforced around us like a shield wall.

The joy of the Lord is our strength …[14]

The truly amazing thing is that it works almost like a magnetic field, pulling others into its influence until the joy and freedom they glimpse begins to dislodge them from the thick, murky darkness of depression, torment, fear, and confusion that has pressed and frustrated them for so long. That first taste of "the glorious liberty of the children of God …"[15] has enough power to unravel years and layers of dark lies. We need to know what we carry, Who lives inside us: the One who is full of joy abides in our inner realms. This Holy One is so powerful He exudes, even gushes, explodes out of us and pulls others into His rich, full love. All this for increase and abundance in our experience of *freedom and joy* …

"… that My joy and delight may be in you, and that your joy and gladness may be of full measure and complete and overflowing."

—JESUS[16]

I teach a class at Bethel School of Supernatural Ministry called "Living a Lifestyle of Healing and the Miraculous." One day, we had a wonder-filled hour and a half, topped off by activation of the eighty or so students and some great healing miracles. After celebrating the breakthroughs together, we were moving like a slow liquid mob of happy humans toward the door of the room when I spied a young man who looked like he needed some joy. I thought to myself, "This guy needs to be drunk in the Holy Spirit." I went over to him, looked him in the eye, smiled right into his face, shook his hand firmly, then held on and wouldn't let it go. I might very well have said something ridiculous like: "Shabba dabba *bam*!" just to prove that it's not the wisdom of man but the power of God. He suddenly doubled over and fell to the ground, convulsing and rolling and laughing until he cried. His friend looked at me wide-eyed and gave me a huge thumbs up. I didn't know what was being set in motion until the following week when they told me this story.

He'd had a nervous breakdown four years before and been chronically depressed for several years, entertaining suicidal thoughts most days for the past three months. Every day was torment for him. On Friday night after the classroom experience, he had a dream in which he had a huge hunting knife sticking out of his skull, and a hand was twisting it back and forth. Then the hand switched to another hand that firmly grabbed the knife and pulled it out. He instantly knew it was my hand that pulled the knife out, and he woke up startled, knowing he had to find me. Certain that I would be in the Healing Rooms on Saturday morning, he jumped on his motorbike and raced to find me, planning to ask me to pray for him. He didn't know it at the time, but his wife went into prayer that night, determined that this thing must end.

The Encounter Room in the Healing Rooms is a huge space filled with several hundred people, a band of musicians playing praises and worship to God continuously for four hours, artists painting beautiful visions of what God is doing, and dancers in a group who twirl and spin and leap about the room with beauty and grace, releasing freedom. It's a place of creativity and Holy Presence. People love being in this atmosphere, and our teams love coming together to create it. This is where this young man came looking for me.

He'd filled out a form stating what needed healing, and he'd written "asthma" because he didn't know how to explain that he had a two-foot hunting knife stuck in his head. (He's a Brit; it's a little weird.) He told me that he was sitting down and saw me walk by, thinking that if I walked by again he would ask me. I was oblivious (which may be pretty common) as I walked about greeting people, watching God move and listening for what He might be saying. I passed the young man again; he chickened out. Several young women stopped by and were praying for his "asthma," but he was agitated and feeling like a failure. I strolled by and saw the man's head bent down, and I stopped and placed my hand on his head and released peace and a blessing. He began to tremble. I moved on. He was now shaking like a jack hammer. He felt a presence and something lifted, but he didn't open his eyes at the time. When he did he told the girls he'd sensed Jesus placing His hand upon his head and that he felt peace like he had never felt before. They told him: "Chuck just came by and placed his hand on your head."

This happened some years ago, and he's come into a greater measure of freedom since then. Joy has been restored, and depression, torment, and suicide have fled! His wife introduced herself to me one day and thanked me for giving her husband back to her. Now, we all know it was God who set the captive free, but the fact that He uses us is a phenomenal joy and blessing. We get to participate in miracles, and we don't even have to know what we're doing. We simply turn our attention toward Him, Him in us and Him in the room. He's here! Oh, how He wants us to recognize that simple truth. And then things happen; that's the way He planned it. *Thank You so much for unending, everlasting, limitless joy that has overcome every aspect of death. You set us free and bring us from death into* life. *You truly are the Living, Life-giving God!*

> "Trust in the Lord with all your heart,
> and lean not on your own understanding;
> in all your ways acknowledge Him,
> and He shall direct your paths."
>
> —SOLOMON[17]

I was sharing these stories at a conference when a father asked me if I would come and pray for his daughter. She had had an extremely traumatic and lengthy labor giving birth to her first child and then gone into severe postpartum depression. It had become so all-consuming that she couldn't do the simplest tasks, overwhelmed by the pressures of everyday life. As she was unable to care for her infant, she had moved into her parents' home, and they were taking over the responsibilities while she struggled with anxiety, exhaustion, and intense migraines. By afternoon, she would have to go back to bed. Even when awake in the morning, if she thought about doing any chore, preparing a meal, or taking on the simplest task, she was instantly overwhelmed by the prospect and immobilized with stress and fear. This was even more overwhelming because she had been a very astute businesswoman and knew what she was capable of. Yet she rarely could pull it together enough to even leave the house. Her husband continued to work and live at their home in another city, coming to her parents' house for the weekends to help out and play with his son. The family was very supportive, but doctors were offering no solutions; a year and a half had gone by and the energy was wearing thin.

When I shared some of these stories of God's miraculous interventions, a fresh hope was kindled. I came into their ample, hospitable kitchen, a room that wore the atmosphere of family and company and wonderful meals prepared and shared. It was warm and homey, welcoming. Daughter, son-in-law, and nineteen-month-old baby were all there, and I asked if I could pray. The young lady and I stepped through the French doors into the green English garden and sat on a bench in the filtered sun. I asked if I could place my hand on her, and she said, "Absolutely." As I turned my attention to Him, the One who lives inside me, and spoke out, "Peace," we experienced a thick atmosphere of holy presence and peace. I commanded the chaos to leave and be replaced by the beautiful *shalom* of Heaven. I kept my hand on her back as it increased in warmth, and it seemed the whole garden filled with His presence. Hope rose up, and glorious, sweet peace was like a fragrance in the garden. I looked at her and asked, "What's happening right now?"

"I can hear a voice saying, 'It's not going to leave,'" she replied. "But that voice is across the garden now, far away, and I can hear a voice inside me saying, 'It's *gone*.'" She told me she felt like she received her mind back. She could think clearly and process. Everything was different. I've stayed in touch with the family, and she has returned home with her husband and child and continued to thrive, living in the peace and joy of Heaven. Her parents, who lovingly gave of their time and care, feel like they also have their lives back. *Thank You God for Your life-changing power that sets people free and restores families to their fullness! You are so good!*

CHOOSING JOY IN THE FACE OF OPPOSITION

I was preaching and teaching with a good friend of mine to hundreds of pastors on the island of Mindanao in the Philippines, sometime around the year 2004. God moved mightily with healing, prophecy, and dramatic outpourings of His Holy Spirit. In one session, we prophesied over hundreds of leaders one by one; it was unplanned and unexpected, but when it began and the flood gates opened up, I can remember speaking words of prophecy to perhaps a dozen of them, and then it was a blur. I realized I had no thoughts of my own and no ideas to fall back upon as hundreds came before me, so I simply opened my mouth, and God filled it, calling forth truth and gifting, callings and destiny for person after person. Many fell out upon the floor into ecstasies as God moved on them, and I have spoken to some of them in the years since then, and they confirmed that God took them into a higher level of calling and anointing since that night. It was marvelous, and I also remember thinking: "I'll never do *that* again!" My game plan now is always to activate *them* to prophesy to each other, removing myself from the equation that leans upon the "Man of God" and placing it back upon every man and woman anointed by God.

The daytime sessions were for conference attendees, specifically pastors, leaders, and ministry students. Each evening, the sessions were open to all to bring the sick, friends who were curious, and those who did not yet know this remarkable Jesus. The Filipinos put on an amazing production with musicians, dancers in glorious costumes, prayer warriors, and a whole team of volunteers. I spoke in the afternoon on the authority we have in Christ—we as believers and followers of the One who has *all* authority in Heaven and on earth. The people were hungry and responsive, and I told them how His authority triumphs over all opposition. Opposition will come, but the greater One lives within us![18]

We left to feast with friends for dinner in a restaurant and take a short time to refresh ourselves before the night session. The conference was held in a school and church compound that took up almost a city block, and it was dark by the time we returned. There were lights on throughout this section of the city, but as we pulled up to the conference buildings, they were all shrouded in darkness—a black hole in the midst of the city. The musicians and sound team were there to set up, but there was no electricity. Power outages were common here. Upon disembarking from the back of the vehicle, we were accosted with urgent concerns that there was no power and the meeting would be starting soon. There was a whole program planned, and people would arrive to a blackened hall. I saw worry, anxiety, fear, and discouragement on the faces of the people who rushed up to us. Many voiced the problem. Then a small band of five intercessors came out of the building and ran up to me, faces beaming with joy, declaring with excited anticipation in their rich Filipino dialect: "Oh, Pastor Chuck, *opposition!*"

Oh, I like *you*, I thought as I invited them into the dark hall and shut the doors behind us. We moved around the auditorium, praising Jesus for His greatness and worshipping Almighty God. The place filled up with joy and peace. Yet I heard the voice of the accuser speak into my mind: "So you're the Man of God who walks in such authority? You can't even make the lights come on!" And he laughed at me. Thoughts, words, and emotions swirled around me, and I had the choice of which to embrace. Anxiety, fear, embarrassment, failure, "What will we do?" and every other form of despair raised its head. I chose with the five intercessors to look into the beautiful face of Jesus, and we worshipped Him, simply because He is worthy of it. As we worshipped, our joy increased, for "in His presence is fullness of joy!" We worshipped not to make something happen or to fight a battle against the power of darkness but simply to worship because He has already overcome all darkness. The enemy battles to see us give up our joy, for he cannot steal it unless we let go of it. After a short time of worship with these five outstanding little ladies, the power returned, the lights came up, and I couldn't even hear that accusing voice anymore as we prepared for an eventful night. Miracles occurred, but the phenomenal and outrageous out-pouring of His Holy Spirit was beyond what I had often experienced. The beautiful dancers in glorious flowing gowns like wedding dresses performed a prophetic dance as brides coming to Jesus that stirred our hearts and brought tears to our eyes. But when the holy bomb of glory hit, I can still see one lovely young lady in her full wedding dress with all its petticoats laid out and flopping on the stage, flipping from her stomach to her back in an almost impossible manner and crying out over the crescendo of the music: "No more, no more, please, no more," and then the Holy Spirit would subside a little and she would cry out again: "No, *more*! No, *more*, please, *more*!" It was the cry of all our hearts that night as we could not handle the surge of presence and power that stirred such wild manifestations, yet when they threatened to withdraw, we could only plead for God to stay and pour out more. It was not the delight in the mani-festations, for some of them were a bit frightening, but the holiness and glory and awe and reverence that accompanied and surrounded them was gripping, and we wanted nothing else but more of the holy fear and wonder of His Presence. At the end of the conference, they held a debriefing at which people shared what was happening to them whilst their bodies were in such a state of manifestations. Each one shared phenomenal stories of encounters with God's love and life-changing power that caused even greater awe to rise up in our hearts toward Him who "only does wondrous things."[19]

JOY WARS

"Rejoice in the Lord always ..."

—PAUL[20]

There are times when joy defines us, when we take it as a military stance against the ravages of circumstance and fear. And there are times we watch our soul's grip let go of it in the onslaught of powerlessness—too much unknown, too much gone awry.

Azi and Mary are Tutsi. That summer, eighty-three members of their family were slaughtered by the Hutus, hacked to death by machetes. We drove through heavy downpours over the muddy roads of post-war Rwanda, peering through rain-soaked windows into the darkness. Our headlights caught flashes of roving gangs, some gathered around fires burning by the roadside. Occasional teenagers in army camo with automatic weapons reminded us of the military checkpoints throughout the trip across the border where they'd emptied and searched our van again and again. The night was thick with tension.

Azi drove while Mary navigated, stress between them rising, the sharpness in their voices escalating, Mary unable to find the house. They were on errand, under the pressure of family and tribal protocol to bless the home of his newly married niece—but darkness, heavy rain, rampant danger, and poor directions presented insurmountable obstacles.

I sat awkwardly in the back seat, watching one of the most loving couples I know fall into a heated argument. While the danger outside was rampant, the air inside the van was heavy and tense and uncomfortable. Then silence.

Suddenly Azi broke it with a shout: "*No!* I will not give up my joy!" Then gently in his rich African cadence: "Jesus gave it to me a very long time ago, and I will not give it away."

Suddenly *Peace* filled the air, as did deep, pervasive *Joy*. The spell was broken. The circumstances didn't change, but Heaven filled that van. With that simple revelation that we have a choice, and with the decision to embrace it, Joy overcame.

PERSPECTIVE

How do You do it?
The way You keep pulling me into the NOW
with these amazing moments that take my breath away.
A sunset …
While the world is pressing and compressing me,
narrowing my options,
just then I step outside
and there it is …
But You'd been spinning it for awhile
while I didn't notice, lost in thoughts; thinking myself asunder.
Suddenly comes crashing in and stops me
with perfect peace …
And wild pinks and purples, gold and orange
explode across the sky …
silently
as sun kisses earth goodnight and sinks
leaving an all-embracing stillness that redefines my heart.
How did You do that?
That subtle way Your love and beauty and extravagance
redirect me.
You are making me resolve to always live in NOW,
that timeless resting place
where war and adventure and striving and compassion
all find their end in You,
and all the yearnings of my heart are stilled and come to rest
as they see fulfillment in the Secret Place
before ever I walk them out in time.
Thank You for making a place for me
in You
so that where You are
I may be also.

CHAPTER 8

ELEVATOR TALES

*"I only do the works that I see the Father doing,
for the Son does the same works as His Father."*
—JESUS[1]

She came into the Healing Rooms with a long list of symptoms, a formidable woman with a strong, take-charge personality. She was well-dressed, commanding, and she wanted to be sure I grasped the severity of her ailments. I looked over her intake form, and there they all were, boldly written out, a lengthy litany of illnesses. I wasn't scanning it to be impressed. I'm really not that impressed with sickness; I'm so impressed with Jesus! I was really just looking for a starting place with her. Halfway down the form was written "Blood Pressure."

"I see it says 'Blood Pressure.' Would you like it to go up or down?"

She looked at me askance, as if questioning my sanity.

"No, really. We can go either way. Whatever you like."

"Well, *down!*" she said curtly. *Are you really this stupid?* is what the look on her face said.

I responded: "There's an elevator button right there in front of you with two choices, up or down. Just push the direction you want it to go."

She looked blankly toward me, a human question mark.

"Really, just push the button. Up or down."

She looked around the crowded room, full of people ministering in groups of three and four. There was no way she was going to push an invisible elevator button, and especially in front of all these people. I encouraged her. I could see she was beginning to lose her control. Very slowly, looking from side to side about the room, she lifted her pointing finger and moved it toward the supposed location of the "down" button. One more sideways glance and she planted her finger decisively on it.

I said: "Going down …" and stepped back. (I never touched her, I promise.) *Bam*! The Holy Spirit knocked her to the ground, and she flopped a bit and then was out. I was sure she was fine in His hands, so I went off to pray with someone else, but I kept my eye on her. After ten minutes or so, I saw her stir and then struggle to get up, so I went over to help her. She was slightly less crisp than when she first came in. I asked her to check out all her symptoms, and she did, but could find *none*! That sly Jesus slipped in and healed her when her guard was down.

And that's what I've found again and again. When we let go of control, when the familiar and comfortable—or even the uncomfortable but very familiar—are moved out of the way, the Healer steps in to lovingly take us on a journey into His heart, in which is healing, wholeness, and all manner of good things planned. We've missed them for so many reasons, but He's never given up. If we can simply help people get their attention and focus off their problems and onto Him who is the answer, the breakthrough comes. But often we can't get them quite that far, from the all-consuming problem to the Answer. The good news is that He is so ready and willing that when we help them just to dislodge a little from being fixated on the problem, He is there to heal them. It's just who He is.

So what's the key? Do we just keep tricking people out of their problems and into healing? Not exactly. Jesus showed us the way: He watched and listened to His Father. He did what He saw and spoke what He heard. And then He tells us He has sent the Holy Spirit, who is watching and listening to Him:

> "But when He, the Spirit of Truth, comes, He will guide you into all the truth. He will not speak on his own; He will speak only what He hears, and He will tell you what is yet to come. He will glorify Me because it is from Me that He will receive what He will make known to you. All that belongs to the Father is Mine. That is why I said the Spirit will receive from Me what He will make known to you."
>
> —JESUS[2]

Oh, and that Holy Spirit lives in *me*. *Oh wait, then I don't have to know what to do?* Right! That's the great news. All I need to do is recognize that He is here, within me and among us. He has a plan, knows the key to unlock any situation, and is completely committed to every person on the planet walking into wholeness, "not willing that any should perish,"[3] in sickness, in poverty, in hopelessness, in despair, in loneliness, in death. He longs for "all to come to repentance," to change our thinking and turn from our focus on sickness, poverty, hopelessness, despair, loneliness, and death toward His promises and His presence, His plan and His purpose, His very nature and character. When we change what we look at and meditate on, we change what we can have and become because truly we must see it first to then participate in it.

What are you meditating on? What, you don't meditate? "Isn't that a New Age practice?" you ask.

Have you ever lain in bed all night, tossing and turning and rehearsing a problem in your life? It could be a financial issue or a relationship problem, a situation at work or in your marriage or with the kids. Yes? Then you are a great meditator.

Now, all that energy and thought you have put into the worst possible scenario playing out gets to be transferred to God working the best possible scenario out, causing all things to work together for good for those who love Him and are called according to His purpose.[4] My goal is to get people's attention and focus off of their problem or condition and onto God and His plan, but most of the time, I am not able to get them quite that far. But He is greater. When their attention is dislodged from the problem for a moment, He is so committed that He slips in and introduces Himself in any of His curious and myriad ways, and the results are heavenly outbreaks of goodness.

Another woman came into the Healing Rooms with an equally long list of illnesses. It seems she had no immunity and simply contracted anything that came along. I was with a friend ministering, and I said to the woman, "Will you step into my elevator, please?" as I held the doors open for her. She entered along with my friend, and I let the doors close behind us.

"Oops, sorry, but all those ailments you had out there got left outside when the doors shut. They're not in here with you. Now, where would you like to go?" I asked.

"To Heaven," she replied.

"Oh, excellent. First, second or third?" I asked, just wanting to be sure.

"Third."

"Just push the button for number three and we're off."

As she did, I began to chuckle with my friend because the three of us were squeezed into what seemed to be a tiny European elevator in the middle of a very large room filled with people. As we ascended, we smiled at each other, but by the time we got to the third floor, the woman had tranced out. She was gone, but still standing. She must have made it to the third Heaven[5] while we were still in the elevator. Suddenly, I began receiving the strangest prophetic words, and I knew I was supposed to speak them to her. I didn't understand them, and my friend looked incredulously at me, her eyes enlarging as she listened to a stream of prophecy that made no sense to us.

I finished, and we waited. In a little while, the woman shook her head and came back to us. "I'd like to go back down now" was all she said.

"Just push number one," I replied, smiling and grinning at my friend and looking for some clues from the woman. She touched the button, and I called out the floors, but as we reached "one," I said to her: "You know all those conditions we left outside? They aren't really yours, and you don't have to take them back when we step out. Jesus has given authority in your body back to you. If they try to come back, you just tell them to leave."

She nodded. When we stepped out, I asked her to check for symptoms, and she could find *none*. She was deeply moved by the experience but not able to communicate well at the time, so we blessed her and said goodbye.

The next day was Mother's Day, and I was on the ministry prayer line after a Sunday morning meeting at Bethel Church. I watched a man coming directly toward me through the crowd of people. He caught my eye and came right up in front of me and said:

"Are you the guy who put my sister in the elevator yesterday?"

Uhh ... maybe. Depends ... I thought as I stalled a little to see where he was coming from—and going. "Tell me about it. How is she?"

"Our mother died two years ago, and my sister has never reconciled with it. She's never been able to release her and get closure. So for the past two years, she has come down with every sickness and disease that comes along. It's like she has no immune system. Today is Mother's Day, and she has been completely overwhelmed this week until she went to the Healing Rooms. When you told her she could go to Heaven in your elevator, she was anxious to see our mom and connect one last time. When you prophesied over her, you said all the things our mother used to say, and my sister was able to connect and finally let go of mom. She came back at peace, finally."

"Wow, that's amazing!" I was dumbfounded at what God had done, and it was fascinating to see how those strange prophetic words fit in.

"My sister came home without any of the symptoms she was previously experiencing. And then last night, they started creeping back in. As she began to complain of them, I reminded her: 'Didn't that guy tell you that when you got out of the elevator you didn't have to have any of those symptoms back?'

" 'That's right!' she exclaimed. And then she rebuked those feelings and all the pain left and has not returned."

Wow, God, You are phenomenal, and You "only do wondrous things!"

Sometimes when the thought of putting someone into the elevator comes to me, I try to avoid it, specifically because I don't want to keep doing something that might become a formula. But hard as I try to resist it, there are those times when it is exactly what I see Holy Spirit doing, and I can't help myself.

A couple came into the Healing Rooms with two teenage sons. The oldest was a great athlete but had come down with some kind of viral infection that left him weak, exhausted, and in pain, unable to play at any sports and barely able to function. His family had been focusing all their time and money trying to find solutions and had found no hope. They were extremely supportive but were wearing down and came to the Healing Rooms as a last resort. So many do …

While praying with them, I noticed the younger brother and had an impression he had something wrong with his knee, so I asked him. He had in fact injured it and was in pain and unable to play soccer, which he loved.

"It's OK. We can pray for my brother. He needs it," the younger one offered generously.

I sensed that his whole life had taken a back seat to his brother's condition for quite some time. He was suffering and he was sacrificing. I prayed for his knee, but nothing seemed to happen, so I prayed again. Nothing.

"Here, step into my pain elevator and tell me what floor you are on right now, with the tenth floor being the greatest pain."

"I'm on the eighth floor now."

"What floor would you like to be on?" I asked him.

"The basement."

"Just push that button and let's go on down to the basement."

He complied and gave me a funny, questioning look.

"Going down," I said as I began to call out the floors: "… seven, six, five, four, three"—I never go above the tenth floor; it would just take so long. "—two, one, basement. Ding! Step on out of the elevator now, please." As he did, he suddenly stopped and said, "No way!" as he bent his knee, put weight on it, and finally jumped on it, feeling *no* pain! "How did you do that?"

I don't know. *How* do *You do that, Jesus? You constantly amaze me!*

I've probably used the Pain Elevator more than any other aspect of this prophetic act. And that's what I believe it is. An acting out of prophecy. I'll define prophecy as this: *to speak or declare the mind and heart of God.* When we see or hear what is on God's heart, like healing disease and removing pain, we can declare it in so many ways: through words, music and song, dance, graphic art—including painting and drawing—and drama, like little acts we do. The simplest might be to make a line on the floor by sliding the toe of my shoe across the carpet in front of someone. That person may have just told me he has been prayed for a hundred times and by the greatest names in healing and nothing has happened.

"This line represents where you are right now. I ask you to step over this line and declare: 'Old things have passed away; behold, all things have become new.'⁶ It's a new day, a day of new beginnings. Everything changes *now*."

I've even had someone who had been prayed for countless times with no results begin to walk in a circle in an anti-clockwise direction as I tell her we are turning back the time until she arrives at the first time she ever received prayer. "Everything is new and fresh. *Now* is your first time, free of deferred hope and unmet expectations. Now I'll declare healing over you like you've never received it before."

There's power in having them engage in the act, a kind of participation that gives them a point of contact, stepping out of identification with the problem and beginning to connect with and identify with the solution. They become part of the healing. Those are words from scripture they are acting out:

> "Therefore, if anyone is in Christ, he is a new creation; old things have passed away; behold, all things have become new!"
>
> —PAUL[7]

As we engage with God's word, His truth becomes entwined with our very being; the words He speaks are Spirit and they are Life,[8] and they become those in us as we become the Word in the flesh. Our participation with Truth as we are declaring and acting it out becomes a dramatic demonstration of that Truth. We are not trying to make anything happen but rather engaging with what is already in the mind and heart of God toward us. It's on His mind and heart because Jesus paid a very great price two thousand years ago that we might be healed.

> Surely our griefs He Himself bore,
> And our sorrows He carried ...
> But He was pierced through for our transgressions,
> He was crushed for our iniquities;
> The chastening for our well-being fell upon Him,
> And by His scourging we are healed.[9]

Matthew tells us Jesus healed all who were sick, and then translates this verse from Isaiah 53:4 this way:

This was to fulfill what was spoken through Isaiah the prophet: "He Himself took our infirmities and carried away our diseases …"[10]

As we recognize and agree with His Truth, what He has done and already accomplished, we end up giving Him glory as we dramatize our thanksgiving and worship toward Him in Spirit and in Truth.

On a trip to Paris, I had taught a Healing School and mentioned prophetic acts, specifically sharing some elevator stories. The next day, we had a large meeting filled with powerful experiences of the Healer moving amongst us. There was great celebration as people experienced freedom from painful symptoms and tried things they had been unable to do. A crippled spine was healed, and blind eyes opened! As we were rejoicing in these miracles, a gentleman came up to me and asked if I would put him in the elevator.

"Sure. Where do you want to go?"

"The Third Heaven."

"OK, just push number three."

As we went up, I asked him what he wanted there. "A new prostate," was his reply. He explained that he'd had prostate cancer and had undergone surgery to remove it, and as a result had become sexually dysfunctional. The elevator stopped at Third Heaven.

"Do you see one?" I asked. He nodded and I suggested he reach up and grab it, which he did. "Just reach down and put it in place …" I said. He did so, and a huge smile spread across his face.

"OK, we can go down now," he said.

The elevator stopped at the first floor, and we stepped out. He shook my hand.

"How do you feel?" I asked.

"Great!" was his reply.

Later that evening, I was at another meeting in a different part of the city. People were arriving and greeting one another when a French woman I'd never met came rushing up to me and kissed me on both sides of the face. "Oh Monsieur, *merci, merci, merci,*" she gushed as she kissed my cheeks again. Slightly taken aback, I looked around wide-eyed, and then saw the doors behind her open … and the man from the elevator with the new prostate entered, grinning from ear to ear, his eyes sparkling. He put both thumbs up emphatically in a demonstration of triumph! *Oh my. That Healer …*

I've even seen whole groups of people have encounters with God in the elevator. I was teaching a Leaders Conference in a small city, and there were around sixty church leaders present. As I was speaking about facing impossible situations, I felt a nudge from the Holy Spirit to ask: "If you are facing an impossible situation in your life right now, please stand up."

I expected a few would respond, but all sixty people stood. *Wow! All right! Got that one right, Holy Spirit.* Then I realized that, of course, they all felt overwhelmed and inadequate. Look at the business they are in: men and women bringing Heaven to earth and changing the very culture around them, bringing hope to the hopeless and displacing a mindset of lack and limitation and filling it with the awareness of the as-yet-invisible, abundant supply of Heaven. Calling those things that are not as though they are …[11] Doing the impossible and seeing lives transformed by God's power. Definitely a job that is bigger than we are …

I asked them to picture the impossibility as a huge, immovable, insurmountable wall in front of them. "Now we are going to move forward with the promises of God. Keep stepping forward until you push right into the impossibility, until your face and chest are pressed into it. And then you are going to keep moving. … The adversary wants you to be intimidated by the impossibility and the overwhelming immensity of the impenetrable wall in front of you. The temptation is to back away, or even turn aside and give up. But we are going to continue to move forward when there appears nowhere to go, no way to proceed. You are pressed to a full stop, and yet you are called to keep moving. How? Oh, look, right there on the wall in front of you, to your right, is an elevator button. Just press it and watch that solid, impassable wall open up into an elevator door to a lift that will take you to the Third Heaven. Every impossibility is an opportunity to encounter God in the Third Heaven and gain His perspective."

I asked them to close their eyes, and they all moved forward as much as they were able in the confines of the seating. Each one then put out his or her finger to press the button. The doors opened. They stepped inside and placed their fingers on Number Three. And then the most remarkable thing happened.

I stood and watched as sixty people stood frozen in their places with their eyes closed and their index fingers pointing into the air in front of them. The Presence of God fell upon the whole room in a thick and tangible way. No one moved or spoke a word. A deep sense of peace and holiness wrapped us all up. Heaven came.

There were children in the back of the large room playing; they became silent and walked up the center aisle and sat quietly on the floor. We were in a public building, and the janitors looked in the doorway and then came inside and sat on a bench against the back wall in complete silence. A holy hush came over the whole place. This lasted for about twenty minutes. It was as if everyone in the room was in a trance except for me. I watched it all in awe, wondering from time to time if I should speak into it. Sometimes our job is to help navigate a Divine encounter, and sometimes our job is to get out of the way. I kept checking in with God to see if He needed any help. It appeared He did not. Though I felt the weighty presence and was overwhelmed by His love and peace and joy, I was fully alert while it seemed the others were not. They all stayed frozen and silent, unmoving. Twenty minutes seemed like forever.

At last, I felt an impression to begin speaking a few phrases of encouragement as several people began to stir as if they were waking from a deep, deep sleep. The pastor who was hosting the event looked up, and I called him forward as we began to welcome people back. There was movement and then some expressions of awe, and when most of the people were fully attentive, one sleepy voice spoke out from the crowd, "Are we still in the elevator?"

People began to share their experiences. My favorite was from a twelve-year-old girl who had been in the back with the children when they came forward. She had gone to Heaven and seen Jesus, and He picked her up onto His lap and then told her some truly amazing things about her identity and destiny, which she shared with us. We were in awe. Some of the leaders said it was the deepest sense of refreshing and the presence of God they had ever experienced. Men and women were revitalized and renewed right in the face of their impossibilities.

"You prepare a table before me in the presence of my
    enemies;
You anoint my head with oil;
my cup runs over.
Surely goodness and mercy shall follow me all the days
    of my life;
and I will dwell in the house of the Lord forever."

—KING DAVID[12]

"Jesus stood and shouted out to the crowds—'All you thirsty ones, come to me! Come to me and drink! Believe in me so that rivers of living [life-giving] water will burst out from within you, flowing from your innermost being!' … Jesus was prophesying about the Holy Spirit that believers were being prepared to receive."

—JOHN[13]

ENCOUNTER AT THE RIVER

I'm watching the river glisten in winter sunshine,
its eddies and swirls, ripples and waves;
its fluid surface pushed yet not defined
by rocks and boulders underneath.
Its river depths so dark and full with motion,
yet all its realms and spaces moving differently:
forceful current rushes through its deepest channels,
while here along the shoreline
and between huge rocky outcrops
the flow seems
still ...
and even gently swirling in reverse at times.
Oh liquid substance of seemingly chaotic motion,
a flow ungraspable, whose current changes with each obstacle
yet never stops,
while on your surface I see Heaven reflected:
trees and sky and clouds,
and over all the shimmering light of sun
casts a million sparkling lights across your rippled face.
Holy Spirit, You play like that with me,
flowing with force and volume over all my deep and rocky places,
and yet so gentle on my banks and in my shallows.
You bring the brilliance of Jesus sparkling across my surface features.
And as the river's mighty flow from distant mountains never stops,
You flow eternally, without beginning and without end:
a love that ever was and never ceases,
that waters all the dry and thirsty world it travels through.
How I wonder at You
living in me ...
flowing through me ...
pouring out all over me ...

CHAPTER 9

THE RHYTHM
OF LIFE

"Are you tired? Worn out? Burned out on religion? Come to Me.
Get away with Me and you'll recover your life. I'll show you how to take
a real rest. Walk with Me and work with Me—watch how I do it.
Learn the unforced rhythms of grace.
I won't lay anything heavy or ill-fitting on you.
Keep company with Me and you'll learn to live freely and lightly."

—JESUS[1]

I was in a huge room packed with joy-filled people who were all excited with expectation for God to move in our midst. A band of musicians and singers led us in hymns and spontaneous outbursts of praises to Jesus, moving in waves and rhythms of thanksgiving, delight, awe, worship, adoration, and explosions of joy. The room was mostly dark, and I moved toward the outer periphery to sit on the floor with my back against the wall. Before me, the silhouettes of hundreds of swaying figures with arms outstretched toward Heaven danced before the blue spotlights in the front center of the room. I sank back into His beautiful presence.

I began to sense a rhythm, a pattern of waves like breathing in and breathing out, systole and diastole, ebb and flow. It felt like we were in the rhythm of all of creation as our worship flowed out into ministry to Him, the focus of all our love and delight. And then came a shift, and I sensed the wave retreating back as we moved into a receiving mode as His love and delight poured from Him and overflowed into us, finally reaching a climax when we were all so full that we overflowed back again into a crescendo of adoration and thanksgiving toward Him, repeating that cycle again and again.

THANKSGIVING

I began to see the ease and rhythm of everything in Him: the pattern of thanksgiving, for example. We recognize His grace poured out, in whatever measure we are presently experiencing, and we respond with gratitude. His grace is a pure, endless, abundant, love-filled river, always flowing from God's heart into our world. The moment we recognize the smallest aspect of God's grace, a pain that diminishes even the tiniest bit, or a financial need for $10,000 perhaps, and we receive $1, we have the choice to look at the vastness of the need that is still unmet or to recognize the first signs of the river of His generosity impacting our need. We can say: "Oh, but I need ten thousand of these and this is but one." Or we can see Heaven opened and cry out: "First of ten thousand, *incoming*! I am a money magnet! Nothing can stop the outpouring of His generosity toward me. The dam has broken, my cup overflows, here comes the flood!"

At the recognition of His generosity, our thanksgiving pours back into Him, and we find that His plans are bigger yet, and then we begin to see the More of Heaven flowing into us, which sparks that response again of gratitude erupting afresh from us toward Him. It is designed to be a continuous cycle of increase, "Life and

Life More Abundantly ..."[2] Glory to glory.[3] Thanksgiving for who He is and what He has promised, given, and done increases our awareness of who He is and what He has done, and thus we enter into and experience more of who He is and what He has done, which erupts in greater thanksgiving until we see even more—and hungering for that more, begin to be transformed as we celebrate the more. It's a never-ending rhythm; it's like breathing in and breathing out. We don't manipulate God to do more by giving thanks. Through thanksgiving, we see that He has already planned the more for us and is wooing us into it, sometimes hiding it and calling us to look for it, to find that pearl of great price He has lovingly hidden for us and from the world.[4] We live in the constant tension of recognizing His grace, celebrating it with thanksgiving, and then seeing that there is more, yearning for the more, and then seeing it begin to manifest, for which we give thanks with joy and celebration as we delight ourselves in Him and His generosity and love for us, at which time we see that there is *more*, He has promised more, He begins to show us glimpses of the more, and then we cry out for it with thanksgiving for we see that He has freely given it to us, and the cycle continues. Perhaps forever ...

GENEROSITY

Generosity is part of the cycle of Heaven that God has initiated. We can make our financial need an event and try to meet that event with Heaven's abundance, or we can realize the abundance of Heaven and overflow with gratitude and generosity. Even our tithes, offerings, and giving can become event-oriented, trying to give to see a need met. How much better to see the pattern, the systole and diastole of giving and receiving and giving again and receiving again. It is actually an aberration of truth that ever causes us to step out of this rhythm and pattern of dancing with God in His goodness and generosity. When we partner with lies of lack and limitation, we pull our attention away from *life* and begin to look into that absence of Life called death.

FORGIVENESS

I saw that forgiveness functions in the same manner. We are forgiven. Out of the recognition of the immensity of His forgiveness toward us, we overflow with gratitude, and then forgiveness flows from us into the world around us. We breathe in His forgiveness and breathe out forgiveness toward others. It is the cycle of the breath of Heaven. When we stop either one of those, we diminish our awareness of *life* and begin to partner with the absence of life and the lies of death.

This is why unforgiveness is so often connected with a lack of health in mind, body, or emotions. When we make forgiveness an event-oriented experience, focused on wrongs and offenses, those wrongs and offenses then become larger than the mystery and wonder of His forgiveness, that forgiveness which supersedes the size and motivation behind any wrong: "Father, forgive them for they know not what they do …"[5]

When focused on the offense, we cry out, "God I don't want to forgive. I can't forgive. She must see how much she has wronged me," and we enter into a justification cycle, leading us deeper into death. However, if we see the value of obedience, we will speak out the forgiveness, even if grudgingly, and God generously pulls us back into Life's thriving cycle. If we live in that cycle and continually breathe in and out forgiveness, when the offense comes—and be sure it will—we are free to love, and we are miraculously able to bless those that curse us and love those who despitefully use us.[6] Creative ideas to bless offenders flow into our imaginations from Heaven!

While camping in the mountains with a large group of friends, we found that an angry group of loud and antagonistic young people were camped nearby. They were irreverent, dirty, and rude, shouting at passersby and throwing rocks and dirt bombs at any who came near their camp. They partied into the night, piercing the silence with their screams and profanities. We had cut and split a huge pile of firewood for our nightly campfires, and while we slept, in the wee hours before dawn, they stole our wood. The next evening, several of us went into their camp with our arms piled high with fresh-split wood.

"We figured you must have burned a lot of firewood as you sure stayed up late last night, so we brought you some more," we told them. We continued to feed them and love them, and they slowly began to respond. They were so used to being rejected that they had adopted the defensive offense to reject everybody else first so it wouldn't hurt as much. But they were still hurting and lashed out from the deep well of that hurt. Our kindness confused them, yet it opened doors of opportunity to talk and share with them. We planted seeds that someone else will harvest.

We have the choice to react to the offense or respond to a continuous flow of God's love and forgiveness. Choices.

When I am locked into judgment toward anyone, I forget that my beautiful savior took all the judgment I deserve upon His own beaten body on the cross so that I am free from judgment, free to be loved. It's true that I've done many things that deserve judgment, and He took it all for me. Now I have the option to take all of the judgment I think you deserve and place it as well upon His precious body on the cross, and then you become free from judgment, free to be loved. We stand side by side, two people standing in a freedom we did not earn and don't deserve. We stand together, loved by the One who gave His life for ours. Forgiven. We're free to now love each other with that same love with which He first loved us.[7] When I live forgiven, I am free to receive love, and out of that love and forgiveness, I am free to love others, and then forgiveness flows with life-giving power because I am in the rhythm of Heaven and forgiveness is the very breath I breathe: breathe in forgiveness from God, His breath, and then breathe out forgiveness toward others, His breath mingled with yours that empowers and anoints yours so that people feel the love and are impacted with Heaven right here in the earth.

WORSHIP

In the same way, our worship to Him can become an event to move His heart, and we worship harder and with greater intensity to see a spiritual, physical, or emotional breakthrough come. But if we recognize that He is already here, within me and among us in the room, and breathe out our joy and delight in Him, then breathe back His joy and delight in us, we abide in that rhythm of Heaven, in the *now* of His presence, in the awareness of His heart already moved toward us and overflowing into us since before there was time. Then we become worship, in spirit and in truth, in fullness of joy, and the delight is not in the event but in the perpetual knowledge of Him in us and us in Him. Intimacy, fellowship, one!

Though we may not initially feel His presence, our very recognition of it based on His word, what He has said, is a form of honor and worship. Our generosity, thanksgiving, forgiveness, and worship are all part of the Divine plan, the cycle and rhythm of Eternal Life, a Life without beginning and without end, not defined or confined to any event but continuously, consistently flowing forever! We come to realize that eternal life is not just a whole lot of time after we die but actually Life outside of time, Life with no beginning and no ending, a continuous river of empowering Life that flows from Heaven, through me, into this world.

HEALING

Healing is much the same. Sickness has that way of pulling us out of our awareness of the rhythm and cycle of *life* so that the disease or pain becomes the event, the focus of our attention. From that place of seeming isolation from the Life of Heaven, we cry out for connection, increasing our sense of disconnection from God, which is all based on sensory input. "I don't feel God; I feel sick and overcome with pain."

But the disconnect is the lie. We can't be disconnected from God—He has moved inside us, closer than our breath; His Spirit living in us gives *life* to our mortal bodies.[8] Whenever the event becomes our truth, we forget about the eternal Truth that we have in Jesus. No matter what the event or situation, the Truth is that He is in us and we in Him. When we breathe that Truth in and out, His breath and our breath, we begin to turn our attention and awareness toward Truth, the One who is the Truth, and His Spirit who leads us into all the Truth.[9] Healing is His name; He introduced Himself to us saying, "I, the Lord, am your Healer."[10] I breathe it in, that breath of *life*, letting healing and health enter and permeate my body. Then I breathe it out into the world and people around me. *Oh God, let healing enter and permeate each person that I come in contact with.*

While we are sometimes waiting to see the full manifestations of healing in our own or others' physical bodies, we must manage our inner world, our hearts and minds, and stay in that realm of truth and the cycle of His life. When conditions or pain persist over a long period of time, the distraction is immense, but we still need to stay in that realm of believing and feeding on the truth. This is when we especially need each other as support in those times when we are in pain, yet holding onto the truth and the life. We are encouragers, sometimes each other's lifeline, and we must never blame or accuse each other for the painful condition we are in.

Although purity, forgiveness, and faith are important assets, if we tell someone it is their sin, unforgiveness, or lack of faith that is keeping them from being healed, we are setting them up to believe that if they can only do something, and do it right, they will be healed.

But healing is not about us getting it right. Healing is a free gift from God that we only receive because *Jesus* got it right. We are here to help each other receive that splendid gift that Jesus already paid for, never to discourage.

"Watch over your heart with all diligence,
for from it flow the springs of life."

—SOLOMON[11]

I have found that when sickness/healing is not a separate, desperate event but rather a violation of God's love that is trying to draw our awareness away from Him who is our *life*, I see more people healed when I stay in the intentional awareness of Him in me and I in Him, established in the rhythm and breath of *life* flowing from God into this world. Let it come through me at any possible opportunity! Let me abide in the Plumb Line of Heaven! Let all the assets of Heaven pour through me into the needy and wounded and hurting and sick all around me, all the time!

CHAPTER 10

BUILDING AN OPEN-HEAVEN COMMUNITY

"... the people who know their God shall be strong,
and carry out great exploits."
—DANIEL[1]

Because of our success in the Healing Rooms, many people come to us asking how to start healing rooms of their own. The problem is that healing is not something we add on to our programs. We know that everywhere there is a great need for it; all of us know someone with chronic illness.

But healing is not peripheral to the Gospel. It's at the very center of it! Healing is intrinsic to the good news that Jesus came and opened Heaven to us—taking away all our sin, guilt, shame, unrighteousness, and everything that stands between us and God, bringing us into the glorious liberty of the children of God.[2] He paid the price that we might come from death into Life, and by His wounds, we are healed.[3]

There was a thief who came to steal, kill, and destroy our health, joy, well-being, hope, future, and access to all the promises of God. But there is a much greater One, an advocate who came that we would have Life, and Life more abundantly.[4] God gave us Jesus that we would not perish—in any aspect of living—but have eternal Life,[5] which is Life without beginning or end, a constant river of Life flowing out from the throne of God.[6]

So my first response to the desire to start Healing Rooms is this: "Do you have a culture of healing in your community?"

What creates a *culture* inside a person or community of people? What causes it to be more than just an event that is miraculous, a healing that happens once or even occasionally? How can we enter and thrive in the very atmosphere of Heaven together, seeing all its benefits abound in and around us?

Our Healing Rooms are a *divine experiment*! We are simply playing with the Truth that we know the heavens are open. We saw in the Gospel of Mark where God ripped open the heavens over Jesus as He stood in the downflow of the Jordan River, the Son, God's pleasure and delight, His beloved, submitting to a baptism to fulfill all righteousness.[7] And since that time of opening the heavens over man, there is no evidence given in Scripture that God zipped them back up again. The veil of the Temple was torn in half, from top to bottom, prophetically displaying that, at the death of Jesus, all access to God's presence was opened to mankind. We can now come boldly before the throne of grace,[8] and we have decided to explore the benefits of such favor.

Our challenge is to get our eight-hundred-plus volunteers to shift their mindsets from having healing events to living in a *culture of healing*. Much of Christianity has become event-oriented, and under an event mindset, we create workers who have to show up for events to serve in various functions to keep the ball rolling. We know we need people and that serving is good and develops great character. But the lie that creeps in is that we have to work for it, it becomes a duty, and we must exercise an act of will to be there on time and give it our best. It becomes more and more about us and our performance, our duty, our will, our need for validation and reward for the great effort we put out. Competition and comparison enter into our Christian ministry! And the more I push myself, the closer I come to burning out. You see, event-based ministry creates workers who need validation and who eventually burn out.

But a culture grows from the inside. We respond to the endless river of His love pouring into us until it pours out in overflow and waters all the dry and thirsty land around us. There is a freeness in the giving out of what we freely receive.[9] A culture flowing from the inside out is a response of love and creates lovers who love the very presence of the One they love, causing them to step out and take ridiculous risks because of love. It's all about His presence, not the task. Whereas workers strive to fulfill the task, need validation, and risk burnout, lovers know they are loved and valued, champion each other, and keep firing up.

We hold events, but we must nurture our people and value those most precious resources to assure that they are not being used to fulfill a purpose but are the very celebration of purpose and an integral part of the open-Heaven community that really is the goal. Here, then, are four things we are continually holding before our people to help keep their minds and hearts focused on *being* the goal whilst we are *doing* the stuff that flows out from the goal. We're learning to shift from a *program*-based ministry to a *presence*-based ministry.

First and foremost, we must learn to *recognize His Presence* among us. We know He is always somehow present, but our goal is to honor His presence, to recognize it based primarily on His promise to be here. "For where two or three are gathered together in My name, I am there in the midst of them."[10] We choose to recognize His presence, interact with the truth that He is here, thank Him for being here, honor His presence even before we experience any sensory manifestation of that presence, and speak to Him—not in a distant, far-away manner, but intimately, lovingly, gratefully, going deeper into every form of personal recognition, respect, honor, and response.

We are not trying to drum up an experience, although it's true that a heightened *sense* or *awareness* of His presence follows the attention we give to that presence being real, here, and now. As we turn our attention to Him, here in the room with us, we want to attune our attention to anything He might do or any way He might manifest that presence. We become aware of peace embracing us, joy, warmth, aromas of Heaven. We want to recognize and honor any manifestation of His nearness that He chooses to display. He will give us impressions, or words or pictures come into our minds— a multitude of subtleties that we learn to be sensitive to so we don't miss the beauty and sweetness of Him in the midst of His people. As we practice focusing our attention on Him all together, we find ourselves falling in love with each other the more we respond to His love for us and love Him back. There becomes a vertical and horizontal aspect of God's love that wraps us all together, and we find a connection that embraces all of us in Him. Our teams spend the first hour of each Saturday glorying in His presence all together before we ever encounter our guests; He is first and foremost. It's all about ministering *from* the place of His presence.

Recently, we were incorporating a new group of seventy-five Bethel School of Supernatural Ministry students onto our teams on a Saturday morning. One of our young men was leading on the guitar and singing beautifully to our King. A couple hundred people moved about the room, singing and worshipping God in the midst of us. The more we focused our attention on God, the more we became aware of His presence. At one point, everyone stopped moving and stood facing the center of the room, many with eyes closed, worshipping Jesus. I stood in the center with a mic and called each one to engage with what was happening, responding to God's love that poured forth, drawing people's attention to each nuance of His presence. The guitar player sang spontaneously and also in choruses all could join, keeping us attuned to God in the midst of us.

As I became more aware of this beautiful unity of the spirit and bond of peace,[11] I also sensed the subtly swirling distractions in the room. Many students were here for the first time. Healing Rooms has a history of powerful encounters, healing, and miracles. There was a slight drone or buzzing behind the glory, a sense of inadequacy, the fear of not measuring up, of being over one's head, out of one's league. I could sense it as a very soft static, as if the station were not fully tuned in. I had to draw our attention to it.

"I'm sensing an underlying fear, the lack of confidence among some of us that we are fully capable, equipped for whatever lies ahead," I said. "If we look at our track record, the failures of the past, the healings that didn't seem to manifest, and every kind of lack and limitation in our faith and possibilities, we become crippled. It isn't actually our faith or our training or our readiness that heals. Jesus heals!

"I want us all to acknowledge those 'little foxes,'[12] but not to empower them. When I count to three, we are all going to make a 180-degree turn away from them and look into His face, His adequacy, His power, His love. Ready?"

Though I had not mentioned jumping and spinning, when I counted to three, most of the people in the room leaped into the air and spun 180 degrees to face away from the center. It was stunning! Immediately, there was a powerful shift, as if a giant torch blasted from the middle of the room, shooting up into Heaven. Worship exploded, and a powerful and pervasive sense of unity came over the whole room.

There are prophetic acts that, though they have no inherent power in themselves, are demonstrations of the invisible Truth that unlocks limitless possibilities. Courage filled the room, as did excitement, even anticipation of triumphs already won. As I stood in the center of the throng, I chuckled at the view as everyone was turned away and I saw the backs of two hundred people all facing outward. Most of their eyes were closed as they poured out love songs to God, yet every time I opened mine, I saw a huge company with their backs to limitation, looking outward in every direction into the unlimited reaches of the abundance of Heaven's possibilities. Wonders happened again that day.

There's a second aspect of presence we teach all our teams that helps to keep us in a *culture* where miracles are normal. It is simply the recognition that he is already here, *living inside me*. Again, we take Him at His word when we feel no evidence of His indwelling presence. He says He's here. We are His temples, and the Holy Spirit abides in us.[13] The Spirit of Him who raised Jesus from the dead lives in me ...[14] As we recognize His presence based on His word, we honor Him. And as we meditate on that truth, we take courage from the fact that the Healer, the Creator of the universe, the living God, is here inside me. How does that work? I don't know, but I dwell on it, thinking about it continually with delight and awe! When impossibility stands in front of me, I stop and say, "Oh, but You're here!" It's a game changer. The biggest shift in my courage and confidence comes when I recognize that He's already here, in me, by His design and plan. Anything is now possible, and I don't have to know what to do. I can simply trust Him, right here in me.

One year, I led a small team of three BSSM students in the Philippines on an outreach. We'd spent the morning going from room to room in a hospital and seen remarkable healing, and then we drove out of town to stop at a small village along the road. It was really just a cluster of shacks, kiosks, and tiny homes surrounding a dirt square where around two hundred people were milling about and doing business. As we pulled our van into the square, the pastor's wife told us they had electricity in this place until 2:00 in the afternoon, and there was a microphone and loudspeaker that probably worked. Would I like to preach to the crowd?

I looked at my watch; it was 1:55 p.m., so I made it brief.

"God loves us so much that He sent Jesus to take all our sin and guilt, sorrow and shame," I said. "He's here now to heal our bodies. If you need healing, come over here, and Jesus will heal you now!"

And that was it. Silence. I looked around the village, and two hundred pairs of dark-brown Filipino eyes looked out of short, brown Asian faces, staring at the four tall, very white foreigners. Nobody moved. There are those times when a minute feels like hours: this was one of those times!

At last, an old woman limped across the square, using a long piece of PVC pipe for support.

"I want to be healed," she said decisively in her dialect.

My team laid our hands on her hip, and instantly she shook and stood up straight, threw down the piece of pipe, and walked perfectly back across the square. There was a gasp, and then each of us was mobbed by about sixty people pressing in for healing. Things happened!

After we saw several healed of pain in their bodies, the crowd around me parted and someone pushed a nine-year-old boy into the center, directly in front of me. He held his right arm tightly to his chest, bent severely at the elbow and wrist, so it looked like a claw. His right leg was also bent at the hip and knee so his foot couldn't reach the ground, and he hopped about like a bird. I tried moving his arm, but it was stiff and hard, and the joints wouldn't budge. I asked how long he'd been this way, and they told me through the translator: "Since birth."

I looked him in the eyes and asked his name; he told me it was Dunker. Placing my hands on his arm, I declared, "Life!" We stayed connected for quite a while as I continued to declare Life and kept my hands on him, moving them up and down his arm.

Many street kids came around, and I got them to declare Life in their language, and they joined in enthusiastically. The crowd was intent, leaning in to see a miracle. Lots of time passed with no change, yet I felt great peace in my spirit. I kept turning my attention to the one who lives within me and felt I had no other words to give than "Life." It seemed to encompass everything, and there was no need for greater wisdom or instruction, just the release of Life. I had a strange sense of direction that seemed to drop into my whole being, as if God were making a deposit into me from Heaven. The thought that came with it was, "I'm not leaving this boy until he's healed." Now, this wasn't a wish or determination coming from my own will, but it was clearly a deposit, as if a gift of faith had been suddenly activated. I've not had that experience often, but I was confident and still, even though, by then, twenty minutes had passed without any change. It was interesting to me that Dunker never got restless or disconnected but stayed with me through it all.

My personal attention span, however, was much shorter than that. As I looked over the entire square, still holding the boy's arm and declaring Life, I remembered that we were on an island that was home to Islamic terrorists known for kidnapping hostages. Two years earlier, we'd been up in the mountains, and Communist guerrilla forces following our exploits had given us only three days to leave the area.

With these thoughts in mind, I realized I was responsible for three BSSM students, and I had no idea where they were. Still declaring "Life," I scanned the village. A tightly knit throng was cheering as an older gentleman jumped up and down with his crutch held high above his head. Matt, one of our team members, was with him in the middle of the throng doing wonders! But there were still two twenty-year-old girls from Canada that I couldn't see.

Searching further, I spotted another crowd, celebrating a miracle in their midst, cheering and clapping. One of our girls was at the center stirring it up! But the other girl was still missing.

All this time, I continued to hold the young boy's arm and declare Life, but my attention was all over the village. I finally spotted a large circle of street kids, with our girl in the middle. She had rounded them up and had them playing "duck, duck, goose," after which she invited them to the church where we were ministering, which was not far down the road. We held a children's crusade the next day, and 150 kids gave their lives to Jesus!

I felt relief seeing all our team accounted for and being their own amazing selves. As I turned my attention back to the boy, I saw that I was moving his arm back and forth, as the elbow now worked perfectly.

"Have you ever done that before?" I asked him through the interpreter. He shook his head to say no.

"Can you do it yourself?" I then asked. I let go of his arm and he moved it back and forth at the elbow as the crowd looked on, aghast.

"Can you raise your arm up?" I asked. He lifted his arm straight above his head and held it there as a huge smile spread across his face, the crowd cheered, and people rushed in to see.

"Dunker, is that really you?" cried a man who had known the boy all his life.

In the midst of the commotion of celebration and questions, the pastor's wife exclaimed, "Look at his leg!" We looked down to see him standing on two identical legs, his feet firmly on the ground! Everyone was in awe.

Just then, several eight-year-old boys ran up to him, pulled him by the arms, and said, "Dunker, *run*!" They pulled, and he staggered a little, and then for the first time in his nine years of life, he ran around the square with the boys!

I was in tears. I still have a photo of him with his arm raised high and a huge smile on his face. In an uncomfortable situation where I had no idea what to do, I could simply turn my attention to the One who lives in me and say, "Oh, but You're here!"

After that, unprecedented healing broke out. The pastor finally had to pull us out of the crowds forcefully and push us into the vans to drive back to the church so we could prepare for the night; he'd made arrangements to bring us back with a band to have an outdoor crusade that evening. It was absolutely remarkable, and we saw hundreds healed and so many give their lives to Jesus. The pastor and his wife then began a Bible study in the village, and it grew to become a church.

These two foundational truths of His presence, among us and within us, lead us into the third key for abiding in an open-Heaven culture as a group, all together going after more. This is the recognition that He is always doing something wondrous, and He wants to do it with me. The Word tells us "He only does wondrous things."[15] He commands us to heal the sick[16]—and the marvel there is that He never tells us how to do it! And when we watch how He does it, He switches it up every time. There is no formula.

The joy we find is in His desire to work in and through us, intimately connected and interdependent. His plan is that we will increase in wisdom and revelation in the knowledge of Him[17] rather than figuring out a method. We have everything we need for life and godliness through the *knowledge of Him* ...[18] He planned it all for a love relationship, and it's only our humanistic mindset that wants to short-cut that precious, ever-growing relationship for personal results. As we abide—stay present, be here now—in His words, we find joy in the ever-increasing revelation that He wants to use us to work His wonders, and our expectation and hope increase as our pursuit of intimacy increases.

A remarkable thing occurs when two or three hundred people come together expecting God to do wonders in, among, and through us. And this is the fourth key to an ongoing open-Heaven community displaying a culture of miracles: We come together with our family whom we love, expecting impossible things to happen. Jesus healed *all* who came to Him,[19] and He said we would do those works and greater, now that He has gone to the Father and They have sent the promised Holy Spirit to be not only with us but *in* us.[20]

Each week, we declare the impossible will happen; each week, we declare *all* who come get healed today. And in those times when that is not what we see, we continue to declare it, to expect it, to gather and prepare for it because it is what He says, and He is the Truth, the living Word, and we are filled with the Spirit of Truth who leads us into all Truth.

So we pursue Truth until there is nothing left but Truth, in the face of all opposition and every obstacle, because we're sure that He who promised is faithful and able to accomplish it.[21]

CHAPTER 11

HOW DO WE DO IT?

"[Not in your own strength]
for it is God who is all the while effectually at work in you
[energizing and creating in you the power and desire],
both to will and to work for His good pleasure ... and delight."

—PAUL[1]

People always want to know just how to pray for the sick and see results. It's not about using the correct formula or words, technique or motions. It's really about delivering a present, a package, and helping the person receive it. It's a gift that was bought by Jesus at a great price through His torture, beating, and crucifixion. He took upon Himself our sorrow, suffering, sickness, and pain, as well as our sin and our shame, so that we can have His Peace.[2] It was a Divine exchange, and it comes as the most extravagant gift ever. Often it is wrapped up in mystery, but the gift wrapping is not the end of the gift. It's designed to be unwrapped.

Just how that life-changing gift is unwrapped is the adventure of our everyday life. We only really live in the present, and we are helping people come back from all their distractions, anxieties, regrets and fears that fragment them into fixating on the past or the future; we're helping them return to the present where their healing (and saving) package awaits them. Jesus inspires us with the many benefits of abiding: fourteen times that word is used in the first sixteen verses of John 15. It means "to remain, be here now, stay present." This is where miracles happen, where Heaven happens.

I've sometimes seen healing like a pulsing, glowing cylinder of light and energy that surrounds those who need that healing. It's usually unseen, but it's already there and available because He bought that gift for us two thousand years ago. The price was paid, and all the work—the craftsmanship—is *finished*.[3] If we focus on the *mystery*—all the whys and why nots—we spiral into a quagmire of debate that has no solution, a series of questions that have no answers. But if we look at the gift that is wrapped up in mystery, we tear right through the wrapping to the present, ready to be revealed in all its glory! Our job is to help that person come back into present time and receive and unwrap their *present*.

I was asked to pray for a family member of some close friends. She'd been a healthy, vigorous, and active woman who had come down with a debilitating disease, something like multiple sclerosis, which caused her to be in constant pain and lose her strength and most of her ability to function. When much prayer brought no relief, she became angry and bitter toward God. Because of my relationship with the family, she was willing to have me pray, but she basically had no faith to be healed. I looked at her and saw how much the Father loved her. As I stepped back to connect with Him, alive in me, I looked about to see what He was doing. Suddenly, I saw a vision of a huge, black plastic garbage bag—really more like a lawn and leaf bag since it was so huge. The bag was suspended in the heavens, packed full and upside down right above her, leaving its mouth at the bottom, twisted shut and tied off with a string that hung down right above her head. I became aware that it was more like a funnel, as the top was open to Heaven, and it was bulging with two years of blessings that had been pouring down from Heaven to her. The mystery lay in why those blessings had been squeezed off to her and tied shut, but I chose to look at the piece of string that dangled in the air above her, waiting to be undone. I described the scene to her and suggested that she just reach up and pull the string …

I should have warned her. Two years of blessings were released all at once! *Bam*! She went down under the impact. But you know, there was healing amongst those blessings. And forgiveness and love and grace and peace, joy, and wholeness. I was simply there to help her receive it.

THE POWER OF THE CONNECTION

The purpose of the whole adventure is *connection*—connection with God and with each other. We are often the vehicle that brings the two together: God's fullness and our friend who is in great need. Faith definitely plays a role here, but it need not be our needy friend's faith. If a person has faith, it is an asset, but she may have none that she is aware of. Jesus praised those who demonstrated faith, but He also healed those who had none or were complaining about their condition.[4] I *might* have the faith to see her healed, but what if I am weak and frightened, never having seen a miracle of the immensity that she needs? Then there is the faith *of* Jesus. Paul the epistle-writer tells me I have been crucified together with Christ, yet now I live together with Him, He in me and I in Him. I now live this life "by the faith of the Son of God, who loved me, and gave Himself for me."[5] He is the Author and Perfecter of faith, even of my faith.[6] And then Paul tells us that this wonderful faith works through love.[7] I see love as the *ability to connect*. God loved people so much He connected with us through Jesus Christ and has now sent us His Holy Spirit to abide in us for the utmost and continuous connection, for "the love of God has been poured out in our hearts by the Holy Spirit who was given to us."[8]

So our goal in ministry is first to recognize our connection with God. I love to stop and turn my attention and affection toward Him, recognizing His presence in me. He tells me He is within me, and I honor His word by recognizing His presence based on that truth, whether I see, taste, smell, hear, or feel Him. He says He's here! The honor of that simple recognition opens up galaxies of interaction. I now understand that I don't have to know what to do or how to do it. He's here. I'm not trying to drum up an emotion but simply recognizing Truth and honoring that truth. I have this connection because of what He has done.

When I recognize my love connection with God, I then turn my attention to the person who needs healing. I connect with her. I like to take her hand as if to shake it as I greet her, but often, I don't let go. I ask her name, then call her by her name and look into her eyes. The eyes are the lamp of the soul.[9] I am becoming the connection between her and God in me. This connection is more important to me than knowing any details of her condition. I may ask her about her condition or not. I may have a word of knowledge for her that God is showing me about a condition in her body she has not yet told me and that He is here to heal. If I do ask about her condition, it is usually to be polite and to get a clear target at which to aim. I don't want a lot of information because I know that the solution is not in knowing how bad the problem is. She may want the empathy of having someone understand her problem, but that will not heal her. Many times, it helps her stay in her problem. If she wants to go on and on, telling me her problems, I will gently *shush* her. It might feel rude, but it's really important. My connection with her is spiritual and physical. The only soul connection that is important to me right then is that she feel safe with me and God. I honor her, but not her condition or the emotional and mental atmosphere that surrounds it. I'm inviting her into the atmosphere of Heaven.

What we do once we have made the connections between God and our friend is impossible to define in detail. Jesus said He did what He saw His Father do. I like to ask Holy Spirit, "What are You saying? What are You doing right now?" It's wonderful when I see and hear directions from Him, but if I don't receive anything right away, I know that I have asked and essentially given Him the "permission" or welcomed His interaction in any way He wants to manifest. I am perfectly happy not to try to orchestrate how He should do His job. I love His surprises!

One time, I was teaching at a healing school where people had asked questions relating to the problem of receiving prayer countless times for a condition and seeing no results. The frustration of it was described by several people, including the struggle of deciding whether to go for prayer again, knowing you believe in healing but every time feeling let down. It is a common dilemma.

I stepped away from the podium and asked if I could use a young man in the front row as a demonstration. He was surprised but willing. I asked his name; we'll call him José. I reached out for his hand and shook it, saying, "It's great to meet you, José, thank you for coming," while I looked him in the eyes. I kept a firm grip on his hand. His knees buckled a little.

"José, we'll pretend you have been prayed for dozens and dozens of times."

He nodded.

"I'd like to brush off of you all those years of frustration, discouragement, and the deferred hope you've experienced. Would that be OK?"

Again he nodded, and I proceeded to brush the debris from his shoulders, back, and head as I spoke to him about letting go of all that frustration. In doing this, I was recognizing his frustrations without empowering them or letting his mind run wild with their influence in his life.

When it appeared they were well dusted off, I asked if he would do a prophetic act for me, and as he agreed, I drew a line across the carpet with my foot.

"This line represents a new day in your life," I said. "As you step across it, I want you to say, 'Old things have passed away.' Then when you stand on the other side, I'd like you to say, 'Behold, all things have become new!' "[10] As he did it, he felt a new freedom, as if something was changing. He was beginning to partner and agree with Truth.

"Now José, I'd like to replace all that frustration and hopelessness with new hope and God's love for you. Would that be OK?"

He agreed, and I placed my hand on his shoulder and the other on his heart and began to pour God's love into him, along with peace, joy, freedom, and a fresh hope. You see, I know I carry those things because of the Spirit and the Kingdom that are inside me. They are the atmosphere and aroma of Heaven, and I can spread them wherever I go.[11] He began to get a little wobbly and started to bend over under the weight of all God's goodness. I asked how he was feeling, and he laughed and gave a thumbs up, unable to use words at that moment. The audience laughed, and I moved him back toward his seat and helped him down as we all applauded and thanked him for his service.

It was just a little role play, a demonstration, but the next day I was being filmed for an interview, and the host called out to the cameraman, "José, did you tell Chuck what happened to you yesterday?" It turned out that he had in fact had a painful injury to his knee and been prayed for many times with no success. He *did* struggle with responding to receive prayer, just one more time, and had pretty much given up hope. When I unknowingly used him as a demonstration, God healed his knee and he now had no pain!

I find it remarkable that often during a teaching session when I use a "volunteer" to demonstrate a word of knowledge for healing, that person actually has the condition and gets healed. *God, You are so invested in our healing and work so independently of our understanding, I am so eternally grateful I get to play with You! Use me again and again and again, please. I'll be the little child anytime and watch You do wonders!*

THE POWER OF DECLARATION

In those times when we don't appear to receive any direction from Holy Spirit on how to minister, we know we can always do a few things. Sickness and pain are violations of God's love for people, and Jesus told us to heal the sick. He came to destroy the works of the enemy, and He showed us that a man can do it because "God anointed Jesus of Nazareth with the Holy Spirit and with power, who went about doing good and healing all who were oppressed by the devil, for God was with Him."[12] Fortunately, He never told us exactly how to do it, no steps or techniques or formulas, so we would always be just as dependent on Him as He was on the Father, for *apart from Him we can do nothing*.[13] So we tell our teams to keep it simple. Tell the bad stuff to *go*, with authority, and then pour the good stuff that's in you into your friend. Do those two things in any way that comes to you, any way that is you, full of Him, dealing with the issue. There's a whole *Kingdom* inside you![14] Plus every spiritual blessing in the heavenly places in Christ.[15] In doing this, we want to always stay tuned to Holy Spirit, because many times He starts showing us what He's doing as we proceed.

We know that death and life are in the power of the tongue,[16] so we always purpose to speak things that are true in Heaven. We are seated with Him there,[17] so we are declaring things *from* Heaven to Earth. Jesus said the words He speaks are "Spirit, and they are Life,"[18] so we are committed to speaking words of Life, life-giving words, whenever we minister.

I was looking at that word for *life*, and I found there are three Greek words commonly used. The first is *bios*. This is physical life, from which we get our word *biology*. Next is *psuche*, the soul life, the emotional and psychic realm. The third is *zoe*, the fullness of life, the life of Heaven. We can speak a different kind of life from each of those places.

When we receive a doctor's report that a loved one has terminal cancer with only months to live, those are *bios* words. They are biological truth according to all the physical facts the medical professionals have. But they are not God's final words, His Truth. And when we receive the medical report, those words affect us at another level. In the *psuche* or psychic or soul realm, those *bios* words impact our emotions, imparting fear, anxiety, perhaps hopelessness, and we then might speak out words that escalate emotional despair. We can admit that the words of biological life and those of emotional life define our physical illness and sick status, along with our feelings of fear and hopelessness.

This is when we must go to the highest realm, the realm where God is, "who gives life to the dead and calls into being that which does not exist."[19] His words impart *zoe* life. When we declare the things that are true in Heaven, they have power because all of Heaven is open to us, and all the authority of Heaven backs us up. The Host of Heaven is listening for those words that *align* with the words of God, for the angels are here to do what He says. We don't command the angel hosts, but we partner with them when our declarations align with what God says, for they hasten to do His bidding.

We don't ask or command God or the angels to do things, but we do command conditions to bow to the one who has all authority in Heaven and on earth, and has delegated to us that authority as His ambassadors on Earth.[20] We tell sickness and pain to leave and declare healing in Jesus's name. "Be healed!" is a declaration that has the power of Heaven within it. So is "Cancer, leave this body now!" As is declaring: "*Life*!" Art, music, dance, and prophetic acts are also declarations that release the life of Heaven when we see what is true there and then declare it on Earth through any of those mediums.

OBSERVE WHAT HE'S DOING

We want to be especially observant of the things that *are* happening when we declare healing over a person, so we quickly ask the friend to take an inventory of their body to see what's changing. I don't ask how their pain is because that is what they are most familiar with, and there may be a residue of it left momentarily with which they will immediately connect and perhaps even magnify through that connection. I ask, "What's *different*? What is changing?" We are looking for any change or diminishing of symptoms or anything new that wasn't happening before, like heat or tingling or pervasive peace. These are all evidence of God working. Just like in the story about the blue sky at the beach where we changed the weather, we want to connect with every evidence of God working and celebrate it. Through recognition and celebration, we honor God as we become more attentive to Him than we are to the condition or problem. Focusing on His world opens us up to greater and greater experiences of His world and all its benefits.[21] He is a rewarder of those who diligently seek Him,[22] and I choose to seek Him out, to search for what He is doing in everything and every place.

A woman came to the Healing Rooms with twenty years of intense migraines. In all those years, she had had little respite from headache pain, and it was impressive to me that she en·ured and kept on going. As we prayed for her briefly, I asked her what was happening that was different. She responded, "My feet are tingling."

"Tingling feet! Yay!" I shouted, but she didn't understand my excitement. Her headache pain persisted.

"He's starting at the bottom and working His way up," I exclaimed with joy as I sought to bring her attention to what God was doing.

As she turned her attention to her tingling feet, she soon shouted, "My ankles and legs are tingling." And soon, "My whole body is tingling!" She continued to experience God's healing touch working its way up from her feet to her head, and then it happened. As the tingling rose fully to her brain, years of migraine pain left out of the top of her head! She was pain-free for the first time in twenty years! *Thank You, Jesus! You do all things well!*

There are times when we pray and declare whilst ministering to someone, and we don't see any change in their physical condition. It's important not to partner with discouragement at those times but to pay attention to whatever God is doing and saying. We always want to leave our friend filled with hope and experiencing God's love. I know hundreds of stories of people healed in the hour, day, or week after receiving ministry. The *why* for that is part of the mystery the gift is wrapped in, and we don't have to understand the reason it happens. But we do want to encourage our friends, to instill hope in them by sharing stories of the many people who have experienced their full healing a little while after receiving ministry.

We believe that it is impossible for us to pray and have nothing happen. So we encourage our friends by letting them know we've just made a deposit into their account and to be looking for the changes as it begins to manifest. Then we want to leave them with an experience of God's love, peace, and joy poured out through us in whatever ways we think of to share those powerful attributes of the Kingdom we always have access to. That's the adventure, drama, and challenge of the present moment for us in closing our ministry time with them. Let's learn to enjoy our interactions with Holy Spirit as we learn to connect with and love the people He loves!

WHAT IS HE ALWAYS DOING?

Somewhere in the magnificent plan of all of this is the wonder that, while God heals, I have a role in bringing it. I am the ambassador He has chosen, "as though God were pleading through us … be reconciled to God."[23] Be reconciled to His righteousness, to His truth, to His plans and purposes, to His love, to His wholeness and His Healing. He is the Savior, Healer, restorer of all things, and yet, in the wonderful plans of God, I am the one who brings it. Each one of us is. And we bring it to individuals lost in guilt and sin and shame as well as to those in sickness and pain and also to people groups and nations, countries and governments of people. We are making unto Jesus disciples of the nations.[24] His message is reconciliation at every level. As stewards of this earth, we bring that message even to the created world, which is waiting in eager expectation for all those sons and daughters of God to be revealed.[25]

"Go into all the world and preach the gospel to all creation."[26]

There are countless adventures awaiting us on the other side of that command!

CHAPTER 12

LIMITLESS POSSIBILITIES

"Do not conform to the pattern of this world,
but be transformed by the renewing of your mind.
Then you will be able to test and approve
[to prove] what God's will is—
His good, pleasing and perfect will."

—PAUL[1]

What if we believed that everything God says is true? Oh, wait … it is true! If we no longer choose to think after the pattern of this world, of lies and lack and limitation, we can begin to delight in limitless possibilities based on promise and the faithfulness of the One who has promised.

I like to take these promises out for a test drive, to prove them. Here's a rather preposterous one I like to test:

"… if two of you agree on earth concerning anything that they ask, it will be done for them by My Father in heaven.

For where two or three are gathered together in My name,
I am there in the midst of them."

—JESUS[2]

Because we lived in the mountains of Colorado for thirty-six years, we've had many experiences with wild, unpredictable weather and found many occasions where we needed to take authority over it and change it. One memorable event occurred on a June morning in 2004 when we were camped at a New Age Festival among twenty thousand countercultural celebrants. A large group of us, consisting of those who knew Jesus and those who did not, were sitting in the open sunlight in a small meadow, capitalizing on the warmth of the mountain morning. We'd experienced a powerful time of worship, with drums and guitars and dancing and singing. I was teaching and leading an animated discussion on life in the Kingdom of God. In the west, there suddenly appeared huge black thunderclouds moving at an ominous speed toward us, and I could see the rain already falling in the distance. Some looked around, and several suggested running for shelter. We were so focused together, and the Holy Spirit was downloading such awesome truth, that I felt to pick up and move at this moment would initiate a scattering that would cause us to lose our momentum and corporate revelation. I felt I caught a glimpse of the heart of God for that moment.

"Jesus said that, when two or three of us are gathered in His Name, He is here in the midst of us, right?"[3] When a consensus agreed, I added, "And that if two of us agree concerning anything we ask, it will be done for us by the Father."[4] Agreed. "So turn around and look at that huge black cloud rolling toward us, and let's command it to part in the middle and go around us."

Those who had been sitting with their backs to it now turned around and looked with shock at the threatening darkness roiling down upon us. We all began to command it to part and watched in wonder as the storm split and the wind blew and it passed around us, leaving us under open skies as rain hit the forest on either side. It actually turned out to be a perfect illustration of our talk on the Kingdom of God and the authority we have in Christ. We'd been discussing the revelations we have of our position as sons and daughters and the promises and authority we have from that position and how the opposition arises in this world toward us as we walk in the fullness of all of God's promises to us.

"… those who receive the abundance of grace and of the gift of righteousness will reign in life through the One, Jesus Christ."

—PAUL[5]

Opposition is sometimes powerful and terrifying, painful and lengthy, but God's faithfulness is always the same, and we need to consistently look into His goodness and promise and not be distracted and overwhelmed, confused or discouraged by the immensity or duration of the attack. It is the thief attempting his steal-kill-destroy program, and our victory is in keeping our eyes on God's "Life and life more abundantly" response. We must realize that we already stand in Christ's victory, and then we make choices from that position rather than striving and struggling to get to it. What the victory looks like can be surprising, especially if we are attempting to figure it out with our intellectual mind or if we expect it to look like we would imagine it. There will always be mystery and wonder in our relating to the Kingdom of Heaven, but He will always keep us in perfect peace when our minds are stayed on Him![6]

In the summer of 2018, we experienced devastating wildfires throughout the state of California. There was much destruction of property and beautiful wilderness areas, as well as the tragedy of lives lost, and our city went through one of the worst experiences of devastation and displacement. Almost a third of our population was evacuated for anywhere from five days to many weeks. There are countless stories of love, encouragement, heroism, and compassion that have changed the fabric of our population, and it has been beautiful to see the city come together and go after rebuilding— but thousands lost everything, and everyone in the city who still has a home knows friends who've lost theirs.

The Carr Fire had been burning since Monday, mostly in the forest, but on Thursday afternoon, it blew up. I was teaching at the Youth With A Mission base on the west side of town, and we all were concerned with the raging sky that engulfed the red ball of a sun. The drama in the heavenlies was remarkable and memorable. At the end of a time of worshipping and rejoicing in God with music and songs, I called everyone's attention to Matthew 18:19 about two of us agreeing on earth about anything and the Father responding from Heaven. "What does 'anything' mean? Really? It's a preposterous promise! Shall we take God at His word? What do you want to agree about concerning this fire?" I asked. There were many excited declarations made to stop the fire, with an enthusiastic consensus!

YWAM fosters an amazing culture of believing God. The more we declared and celebrated God's offer of promise and truth, the more our faith seemed to expand and our excitement grew. Around eighty of us turned toward the west and commanded the fire to stop and turn away from the city, and there was a powerful time of agreement, with declarations made, celebration, shouting, unity, worship toward Heaven, and great joy. Those with the faith to see every impossible situation bow to the name of Jesus lent an authority that encouraged others to step out and trust God's promises toward us and agree with them, which empowered others who were less confident to jump in and take courage, proclaiming the desires of their hearts to a very present God, right in the face of danger. He surely prepares a table for us right in the presence of our enemies[7] to display His love, favor, and power toward us when things look hopeless. He is the God of all hope who fills us with all joy and peace as we believe in Him so that we abound in hope through the power of the Holy Spirit.[8]

At the end of the meeting, people came running into the building to tell us all to evacuate. A rare phenomenon dubbed the "firenado" had jumped the river, our major barrier of protection, and a consuming blaze threatened the entire city. Firefighters had to retreat, and Interstate 5 was the next hoped-for line of defense. Mass evacuation of the entire western side of Redding was underway, and the roads were gridlocked with vehicles taking up all the lanes on every route coming out of the hills around the lake in a creeping escape from swirling funnels of flame and billowing smoke clouds as the crimson ball of the sun sank into the west. It felt like an apocalyptic movie scene as we moved eastward at a snail's pace along Highway 299, heading downtown with fiery terror filling the sky behind us. All around us were vehicles of escape: some had had time to pile up as many personal belongings as they could while others had only the random bike or tools thrown into the back of a pickup. It took two hours to go only a few miles, and when I got to my turnoff, there were barricades and police forbidding entry into my sector. I'd had intermittent phone communication with Linda, who was loading the grandkids into her car to move to a friend's house on the east side. Our daughter Grace was trying to get back home to the kids; fire was burning at the end of our street. Everything seemed in chaos.

I tried several back roads to get home, wanting to pack up anything important, but all traffic was one way out with no passage in. I was pushed along by bumper-to-bumper traffic until I finally was able to make the entrance ramp to I-5 South, where vehicles were actually moving at a more reasonable speed. I called several friends who were also evacuating until I found one in the southeast sector who welcomed me for the night to join them and their five kids, plus a houseful of refugees. It was something of a party, which we all needed at that point.

I was able to get through to Linda and found she and Grace and our four grandchildren were all safe in our friend's large house, so I planned to meet them in the morning. As I lay awake on my good mate's child's bed, thinking over the events of the night, I held onto the Father as I consciously let go of my home and each item that was important to me, realizing I might never see them again. I thanked God for the truly important thing: the safety of my family.

In the morning, Redding was like a ghost town, with no vehicles on the roads as I drove around detours to get to our house. Electricity was out and traffic lights dead. Home was there, and it appeared to be outside the perimeter for the time being, so I packed the contents of both our refrigerators and freezers into two large ice chests, grabbed important documents, clothes and toiletries, and drove over to my family. Later, Linda and I returned. The power had come on, so we turned on the sprinklers to water lawns and bushes, hosed down the roof and trees, and prayed over our property. It was five days before we were allowed back in, and the National Guard came to man the barricades so we couldn't sneak across.

We found that the fire had turned back away from town shortly after our prayer time at YWAM. I know many others also were also praying and Heaven intervened: the fire line had crossed all containments and was devouring the western subdivisions with no sign of letting up, yet it miraculously turned and moved back into the forests, though doubling in size. I was interested in getting back to YWAM to see how they reacted to all that had happened, and I was glad to see they saw a victory in the turning back of the fire, even though we did not see it completely cease.

It's so important to recognize and celebrate the things we see that God is doing and not stumble over the things we do not yet see completed. It's also important that we not get bogged down in the unanswerable questions of "Why, God?" but hold onto that promise and faith against all odds and every opposition, never dragging the truth of His Word down to the level of our experience by making up doctrines to rationalize why we do not see things happen. We must stand together on the truths of His Word and promises with endurance until all our experiences finally come up to the standard of His Word.

By Sunday, the fire officials gave permission to gather at the church, and it was so good to worship together and turn to God as one body in the midst of all the chaos. Every greeting and hug came with the question: "Are you home? Do you have one?" We loved and prayed for those who'd lost everything and manned a trauma ministry room to love people through their crises. In the afternoon, Bethel became a Salvation Army Distribution Hub, and within hours, hundreds of volunteers—many of them evacuees themselves—turned grief into loving service, preparing rooms with tons of supplies for distribution the next day. It felt life-giving to move from survival to service. We continued as a distribution center for two more weeks and then moved into the ash-out phase.

What a joy it was to finally see traffic on Lake Boulevard, with the barricades *gone*! It felt like a city again instead of a war zone. On the fifth night of evacuation, we slept at home in our own bed! *Thank You, Jesus!*

Over the next weeks, many of us spent days in hazmat suits "ashing out"—sifting through the ash and debris of burnt-out homes. What an honor to serve those precious homeowners who had lost everything. We found many forgotten treasures, and I found four diamond rings, helping families find connection to a lost past, closure in a devastated present, and hope for a future of rebuilding and restoration. As we prayed with them, I was humbled and honored to be part of God's Love extended in this way.

It felt pretty surreal to return to some levels of normalcy while the fire still burned near Lewiston. I finally had my first opportunity to take time off to mow the lawn in the early-morning cool, wearing an N-95 respirator while knowing many friends no longer had lawns to mow. Someone's roof shingles were floating on my pool, and ash and charred wood was on all the outdoor furniture. When sections of the city opened, I was able to go in with my friends to view for the first time their leveled homesites. More prayers were needed! The opportunities to love were unlimited!

I believe we are here to bring Heaven and its peace, hope, and promise into every sort of disaster—from wildfires to family break-ups to victimization and abuse. All have lasting after-effects of destruction and trauma, but His love is able to carry us through and heal us. In whatever way the thief comes to steal, kill, or destroy, we become part of God's plan to bring Life and life more abundantly.

Many who lost homes were shattered by the loss, and others immersed themselves in His grace to stay above the stormy whirl-winds of emotion while still grieving. But we're seeing stages of grief coming in waves as time passes as the need to rebuild with all its emotions and decisions hits, as memories are triggered. Heaven on earth doesn't negate grief and loss, hardship or even betrayal. Jesus bore all of those for us that we might find a very present refuge in Him when every storm hits.

I'm still growing and working to see an end to destruction in all its forms, from accidents to sickness and disease and to disasters of nature and weather. Sometimes, changing the weather is for fun, and sometimes it's to relieve destruction. Sometimes stopping a fire can be instantaneous, or it might turn away but take weeks to go out. We're learning to intercede, to stand between our people and disaster, to change the weather, to stop storms and call out the sun. I feel like I'm in training because there's a great need for us to grow up to stop hurricanes, tornadoes, typhoons, and all injustice, to bring an end to every violation of God's love perpetrated against every person, from acts of violence to slavery to forces of nature gone awry. We each need to start somewhere! And whilst learning, we continue to minister hope, comfort, and love in the wake of every storm.

CHAPTER 13

TAKING IT
TO THE NATIONS

"All authority has been given to Me in Heaven and on earth.
Go therefore and make disciples of all the nations, baptizing them
in the name of the Father and the Son and the Holy Spirit,
teaching them to observe all that I have commanded you;
and lo, I am with you always, even to the end of the age."

—JESUS[1]

I've traveled and ministered in thirty-six countries, including spending a month in Europe in the summer of 2010. At that time, I experienced a fresh stirring in my heart for those nations. I felt pulled; I wanted to go back. I'd been in England, Belgium, Germany, Finland, and Russia before, but that summer in Switzerland, Germany, Norway, and Sweden, I met people hungry for an encounter with the Living God everywhere I went.

I kept thinking about France. If Europe was this ripe, could it be time for France? I don't know what it is about France that draws me to it like a lover, but my imagination has drifted there for years. My hands have traveled the map from Paris to Provence, from the Atlantic coast to the Mediterranean, the Pyrenees to the Alps. I'd never been there and knew no one who lived there, but I kept dreaming of opportunities. Something I love to do is go to a place where I know no one, have no connections, sometimes can't even speak the language, and plant my feet on the soil of the land, and watch what God will do! I know He is ultimately invested in all people in every land; He's the Loving Father with a heart bigger than the universe toward us, and He's only looking for sons and daughters to step out and let Him lead them, to stand under an Open Heaven and let Him pour out grace and love, healing and salvation in new and unique ways. I wanted to stand on French soil in awe and wonder and see what He would do with me.

A chance to travel with three people I really like to the UK came up in the spring of 2011, and I pounced on it. We'd spend two weeks holding healing seminars and preaching in England, ending with a conference on the Island of Guernsey before the team flew back to the States. As I looked at the map and saw only about fifteen miles of water between Guernsey and France, I decided not to book a return flight with the others to the US but to take a boat to the port of Saint Malo on the West coast of France. I had very little money and knew no one there, but I figured I could catch a train to Paris, where I also knew no one. Reasonable plan. I decided that staying a week would be perfect.

Something about landing on the soil of the country fascinated me, and I knew that when I arrived, wondrous things would happen. When I talked to the Lord about it, He seemed delighted. I felt a kind of intercession being birthed in me with the thought of just planting the soles of my feet on the land, on French soil, and being an Open Heaven: the son on earth standing in alignment with the Father in Heaven, letting the presence of God who lives in me, the Holy Spirit, connect with God's presence both in Heaven and in the land, to be in the plumb line of Heaven, like that lightning rod, grounding all of Heaven's resources to add fuel to some as-yet-unseen fire in France. I was sensing He'd been stirring things there and I had the privilege to be a part of something He was doing. It was very vague, and yet in a strange way substantial and mysterious, but perfectly logical. It's the kind of passionate, irrational behavior that attracts miracles. I sensed God was leading in it, and I couldn't wait to see what would happen.

The more I plotted a train and bus course from Saint Malo to Paris, the more logistically impossible it became. I wanted to stop at Mont Saint Michel and explore, but bus and train schedules were not meshing. I set the plans aside and talked to God about what I would really like to see happen. Here's my personal dream list:

> *I want to invade France by boat, set my feet on the soil of this country, and be an Open Heaven and see what God will do.*
> *Visit Mont Saint Michel.*
> *Meet Healing Revivalists from all over France.*
> *Teach a Healing Seminar in Paris.*
> *Preach in a church in Paris.*
> *Stay in an apartment in the center of the city right across from Notre Dame. I picture an old, top-floor garret room with a window that looks out over the rooftops of Paris, from which I can walk about, exploring the heart of the city day and night.*
> *Have someone take me on a tour of Paris and show me really special places that tourists might not see.*

I asked God what He thought about it. "Sounds like fun" was His response! I had a sense He was more invested in it than I knew, and this increased my level of curiosity and excitement.

Suddenly, I began to run into a few people at Bethel Church with some serious French connections. Outstanding things opened up. First, an amazing woman on staff randomly asked me if I had ever thought about France.

"I'm going there in two weeks!" I exclaimed.

"Who do you know there?" she asked.

"No one …"

She had lived in France and told me she had friends, Arno and Margarete, who lived near Saint Malo. She thought we'd get along superbly and even felt I could be a great encouragement to them at that particular time in their lives.

They emailed me and said they were traveling to Paris the very morning my boat docked and would love to pick me up; we would drive right by Mont Saint Michel, and they'd be happy to take me on a tour of the walled-island monastery-mountain fortress. There was only one catch: they were driving up to a meeting in Paris that night and insisted on taking me with them.

"Oh, what kind of meeting is it?" I asked.

It just happened that a group of radical revivalist forerunners in the Holy Spirit, healing, and miracle stream in Europe were coming together in Paris that night for an informal meeting to connect and fall in love. And they insisted that I join them.

What are You setting up, God? Is this You birthing all these desires in my heart? I had been reading about Abraham and Moses; the Bible says they were God's friends. "I want to be Your friend, God," I had said. *Is this how You play with Your friends?*

The next day, one of the first French students at BSSM came up to me and said he'd heard I was going to France. He asked if I would like to preach in a church in Paris.

"Why, yes, I'd love to …"

He phoned his pastor, who asked if I would be willing to teach a Healing Seminar on Saturday and then preach Sunday morning in his church.

Wow, God! I'm overwhelmed by You!

INVADING FRANCE BY BOAT

There was one more initial obstacle: I didn't have money for the boat fare from the Island of Guernsey to Saint Malo. I had emailed an old schoolmate who lived on the neighboring Channel Island of Jersey to see if he might pop over to Guernsey for our conference. He was keen, yet later emailed to say he couldn't make it but wondered if I'd be open to visiting him and meeting his prison ministry team, praying together, and catching dinner. In return, he said, he'd like to host me for the night on Thursday, paying my boat fare from Guernsey to Jersey, then on to Saint Malo Friday morning. I had told him nothing of my need. *Oh God, You're perfect!*

We sailed through rain, clouds, and mist as I left the Island of Jersey with its medieval castle fortifications fading into shadows. Though its surface was pummeled by rainfall, the sea was relatively level, the big ship barely lurching in its stride across the water. As the rain lightened, gray-shadow islands appeared on the horizons, along with sailing vessels, and I was in awe of the misty beauty of sky and sea and land, like a stunning watercolor painting that captivated my soul. And then, appearing like a dream as the sun broke through the fog, there it was in all its splendor: the walled pirate city of Saint Malo. The massive stone fortress completely surrounded the small city as it rose directly from the rocky coastline. Everything seemed to want to grow upward within the constraints of the walls, and the rooftops, towers, and church spires reached well above the battlements into a sky whose clouds were breaking open to let the April sun shine through. I was captivated by the rugged solidness, stunning scenic impact, and historic romance of the place. A pirate city …

THE WALLED PIRATE CITY OF SAINT MALO

Arno and Margarete met me as I docked and asked if I'd like to check out the city. *Are you kidding?* As Arno parked the car, I bolted for the huge medieval towered gate that rose up from the cobbled street, right across from the three-masted schooner that towered in the harbor.

The portal was cavernous, pulling me into its jaws as I looked around at the massive stonework. *Who has passed through these gates before me?* I was suddenly funneled into narrow cobblestone streets walled in by ancient tall buildings that virtually blocked the sun and filled the sky like grey stone canyons. Winding through the constrained passageways, I headed for altitude and daylight, which finally brought me to the top of the fortress wall that embraced and contained the tightly knit city. I breathed the salt air and explored the ramparts, catching the stunning westward view of the rocky coastline that plunged out into the sea, topped in the distance by a smaller walled fortress. It was the stuff of heroes and legends.

This was the place where my feet first touched the drama that is France. History and Heaven intertwined with people and their culture streaming through the ages; medieval beauty intermixed with twenty-first-century technology, all resonating under Heaven, sparking an intermittent connection that called out for jump. I felt I was here for such a time as this, my feet on the ancient stones and soil of France, aware of the eternal Spirit within, connected to the Father and Son who reign in eternity over all creation, standing in the Plumb Line of Heaven on behalf of all of France, part of a divine master plan to awaken a beautiful, cultured people to the glory that is God among us. I had no idea how to do that or what it would look like, yet I knew the land itself was groaning, waiting for the sons and daughters of God to be revealed ...[2]

LE MONT SAINT MICHEL

You can see Le Mont Saint Michel for miles as it rises up from the low-lying coastline. Mile after mile, it grows in size and splendor as you drive through the French farmlands, until at last you can see the golden statue of Saint Michael with his trumpet shining in the sunlight atop the towering spire that crowns the cathedral at the pinnacle of the rock fortress. It is impressive.

We toured the citadel and had a lunch of crêpes, both savory and sweet, on an ancient balcony in the tiny walled city. I was infatuated. Then we passed a shop that displayed all manner of weaponry, from knives to swords and medieval lances and bows. It's one of my love languages. As I glanced into a glass case, I spotted one particular knife that was exactly like my favorite pocketknife, which I had lost on a missions trip a year before. I had called it back, but it had not responded—yet here it was inside this case in a medieval village in France. I was stunned. As I stared at it, Arno came up to me and asked if I liked the knife, so I told him the story. As we left the shop, he presented me with a small package, and I still have that knife to this day. *Oh God, is this how You play with Your sons and daughters? You care about every detail of our lives. I am stunned by Your goodness and love.*

ON TO PARIS

It was nightfall when we drove into the beautiful city lights of Paris, circling a few times around l'Arc de Triomphe looking for one of those streets that spread out like the spokes of a gigantic wheel from the hub that is the roundabout encircling the monument. We parked on an avenue of palatial buildings and found our way into their good friend Kelley's dance studio, which had once been the horse stable in the courtyard of a splendid, gated mansion that now was divided into many elegant apartments. And once inside, I met my people: French, German, Welsh, Scottish, all infatuated with Holy Spirit and His plans for mankind. There was immediate camaraderie as we fell in love, drank of one Spirit, told tales, and laughed a million laughs. Languages and accents overlapped; some needed translation, but the common joy didn't and was freely understood. We spent the evening sharing our stories and hearts, our passion and prayers, eating and drinking, and drinking again and again of Holy Spirit's Joy. Late in the night, a group of us drove to Kelley's spacious house outside the city and stayed up until the wee hours becoming family.

God is connecting His people all over the world, in the smallest and greatest ways, preparing us for such an outpouring of His grace and love that no opposition can withstand it. We need only to respond, to fall in love with those He brings to us, to let Him build His church from every tribe, tongue, and nation. Pay attention! Don't miss the importance of the connection that is right in front of you.

In the morning, Kelley and her sister Erin drove me to the train depot to catch the commuter back into Paris to connect with my host for the Healing School that day. We met at a tiny restaurant, where I feasted on a most memorable and succulent roast duck smothered in blackberry reduction. I love France!

The pastor was expecting a much younger man, as he was thinking in terms of his own student at BSSM. I was expecting a Frenchman, but found a Brit who pastored a charismatic French church. We were both surprised.

MIRACLES

The Healing School was well attended, and after a time of teaching, I paired everyone up to practice on each other. Some wonderful healings occurred. I remember an ear opening up to hear, long-term pain leaving, and many other breakthroughs. My translator was a lovely young Frenchwoman who asked me where I was staying while in Paris. When I told her "With the pastor," she replied, "Oh, but he lives way outside the city. I have a tiny flat on the top floor of an old building in the Saint Michel region, directly across the river from Notre Dame. You will be able to walk about and explore the heart of the city. I will move in with my friend, and you can have it for the next four days."

We climbed five flights to the top-floor studio, and I looked out the single-gabled window to see the Eiffel Tower lit up and sparkling over the rooftops of Paris—exactly what I had put on my dream list. *Thank You, God. You are so wonderfully thoughtful and caring toward us!*

The next morning, the church gathered in a large rented space in a fine building with a long lobby through which people streamed from several directions, funneling into the room, bringing a joyful air of expectation. The seats were full, and the music team was quite good. As we all stood in a lively and celebratory worship, I had a sudden awareness that Holy Spirit was ready to break out in our midst. I moved around to the front of the auditorium where the pastor and his wife stood with hands raised, and I pulled them both into my arms in an embrace and spoke into their ears, "He's here!" And then I said something in an unknown tongue, and they both dropped to the floor shaking. She later told me she turned to her husband and said, "Oh dear, we've unleashed him!"

I felt the electricity of His presence powerfully in the room, and with no plan at all, I headed down the center aisle, touching people on both sides, and they shook, fell back into their seats or to the floor, laughing, shaking, shouting, and manifesting many responses to a powerful touch from God. As the music continued, I began to climb over chairs as I felt He wanted me to reach people in all the sections, and when I made it to the back row, there were all my revivalist friends from Friday night, rejoicing and adding to—perhaps multiplying—the level of wild and abandoned outpouring. The pastor's wife spoke out over the mic from her position rolling on the floor, "If you want to experience an increase in the intensity of God's presence, come up here to the front. The anointing is powerful here." Many flocked to the front. This proper British pastor's wife moved toward the stage but then fell backward onto it, kicking her feet in the air. As she caught her daughter's eye in the congregation, she could only shrug her shoulders and point up to Heaven as if to say, "This has to be God!" Her daughter, knowing her mother's disposition and personality, shrugged her shoulders and pointed up in agreement, declaring: "This has to be God!"

People who came forward began to experience healing as well as other aspects of His presence, and there was much ministry and loudly wild celebration of thanksgiving for what was happening in our midst. After a short preaching of God's Word, I called any who still needed healing to stand and asked all the others to gather around and release the healing power of Jesus that was so present among us.

Fantastic miracles occurred. One woman who had arrived wearing dark glasses and walking with a long white stick such as the blind use to feel their way along was the center of some loud and triumphant celebration. She then came up to me without her dark glasses and presented me with her walking stick as a trophy of God's Grace, praised His goodness, and walked home unaided! Another woman, the mother of six children ranging from around twenty down to childhood, had a severe degenerative spinal disease that caused constant and intense pain. She was in need of surgery and a fusing of her spine, but resources were slim. She could barely move, the pain was excruciating, and her children huddled around her in grief and fear. Suddenly, all the pain left, and she raised her hands in the air and danced about, praising God. Her children hugged her and wept for joy. God's presence and power were so obvious in our midst that nothing seemed impossible!

The music team had returned to playing joyous, exuberant praises, in which everyone joined as we celebrated and rejoiced over the wonderful breakthroughs happening all around us.

People's lives were changed; pain and suffering had fled; glorious healing and hope had displaced desperation and disability. As the crowd began dispersing, there were many embraces and cheeks kissed in the French manner while we separated to take our afternoon meal. Two sisters came up to me to ask if I had plans for Monday, saying the Lord had impressed upon them to take me on a tour of the city, showing me special highlights I might not otherwise see. *Oh Lord, You embarrass me with Your goodness toward me!*

The pastor hosted me again two years later for a night of healing training while their son and daughter both attended BSSM in Redding. I was delighted to see the parents join them in another few years, completing first and second years in our School of Supernatural Ministry and serving in the Healing Rooms at Bethel. Family transformation is a beautiful thing.

ABUNDANCE

The next three days were a riot of beauty and delight, of architectural splendor, outrageous five-course meals, and museum intoxication—I was overwhelmed by the physical intensity of all my favorite Impressionists under one roof in the Musée d'Orsay. All of this coupled with a welding of friendships with fantastic people. Some of those from the Friday night gathering subsequently opened doors across France, and I began taking several trips per year into this beautiful country, holding healing and Kingdom-culture conferences and seeing so many people encounter the Holy Spirit in new and phenomenal ways. God had a plan to bring His church in France into greater levels of joy, and invited me to join Him. I recalled the prophetic word I was given in England the week before, where a couple saw me driving a donkey cart across the land of France with a humongous wine barrel mounted on the back, tap open, dispersing the new wine of the Holy Spirit from city to city. *Yes, please! If this is what You are doing in France now, God, I want to be a part of it! You've called me to be a "Broker of Heaven."*

One of my favorite healing miracles occurred the next year when I was invited to hold a conference in a small city in southeastern France. The whole conference was a three-day explosion of joy and healing, and so many French men and women littered the floors as they experienced God's presence in powerful ways. On the third day, I came upon a young man still standing who'd come for healing of his back. He was in the French Mountain Brigade, a kind of special forces that ski over the Alps carrying huge backpacks and scale the faces of giant dams, involved in all sorts of extreme adventures. However, he had injured his back so severely that he couldn't continue, and he was scheduled for surgery and a spinal fusion. The pain was intense. When he came into the conference, he saw many people getting healed and many experiencing great joy. He wanted both. On this third day, I thought he must have been healed and asked him how his back was.

"It's so painful," he replied.

I had a sudden flash of God's heart.

"I'll tell you what we're going to do," I told him, motioning to a tall bistro table nearby. "You're going to lie down on the floor, and I'm going to get up on this table, and then I'm going to jump on your back and God's going to heal you!"

His eyes were wide open as he replied, "I need a translator."

Actually, his English was very good, but as he searched for the translator, he found her laughing uncontrollably on the floor in a pile of extremely happy people. He returned.

"Did you say, '*I* will lie down on the floor, and *you* will get up on the table and jump on my back'?" he asked.

"Yes!" I said. I didn't touch him, I promise, but he was suddenly thrown backward about six feet, landing on his back on the floor and then he flopped around a bit, laughing hysterically. He lay there for about ten minutes. When he began to stir, I went over to him and helped him up.

"How's your back?" I asked, and he twisted and turned and then bent over and touched his toes and came up again, all with *no pain*!

My wife, and some others as well, have asked me, "What were you thinking?" Actually, I wasn't thinking anything. I just had an impression. "Would you have done it?" I don't know—I never got that far or thought it through. Sometimes, I just feel God's heart and have to respond. I do think Holy Spirit got on the table and jumped on his back on the floor. I guess I was just saying what I saw Him doing, just like Jesus.

The next week, they canceled his surgery because there was no longer a problem, and I've stayed in touch with him via Facebook and the internet. He's gone through officer training school and married the beautiful young lady who was his girlfriend when I met him. His life has been changed forever by the hand of God! Eight years later, he surprised me, showing up in a meeting in another city in France where I was preaching. We had the joy of reconnecting and celebrating that he has had no issues with his back in all those years! *Thank You, Father, for all those lives I've seen You change since we first adventured into France. I love Your ways!*

Back to my first trip to Paris. When, at last, Wednesday came and I had to leave the City of Lights, I took the high-speed train to London that tunnels under the English Channel. In the comfort of my seat, I reflected on all that had occurred and how gloriously God had healed people, touched many lives, and fulfilled every dream and desire, exceedingly abundantly above all I could have imagined. I pulled out of my jacket pocket the knife and a variety of envelopes that people had given me through the week, and found in them a total of four thousand euro!

I was overwhelmed with gratitude, and I heard Him speak gently and lovingly in the quiet of my heart: "This is how we'll do trips from now on."

Oh God, I am undone by Your kindness and generosity toward me. It's true that "Your gentleness has made me great ..."[3] *You are a good, good Father, and I truly am the son whom You love. Thank You! I want to always be a part of the wonderful things You are doing in the earth!*

FIRE, WIND, WATER, EARTH

Thank You Father
for the fire that lights up the sky:
the sun, with its sunrises and sets,
the moon and stars …
and the flash of lightning
with thunder that speaks from Heaven.
For the tropic storm,
the cleansing, drenching rain,
the beautifying shower.
And thank You Father
for the wind that drives us,
carries us, gives us movement, speed;
for the joy of motion, our adventure.
For the sea that embraces us
the pulse and swell and heave
of her great blue depth—
our course and our ride,
our playground.
For the earth that becomes our anchorage,
our mooring and shelter,
our destination, delight, and discovery,
our Safe Harbor.

CHAPTER 14

SAILING THE CARIBBEAN

*"Suddenly they heard the sound of a violent blast of wind
rushing into the house from out of the heavenly realm.
The roar of the wind was so overpowering it was all anyone could bear!"*

—LUKE[1]

*"Then, like a wildfire, the Holy Spirit spread through their ranks,
and they started speaking in a number of different languages
as the Spirit prompted them."*

—LUKE[2]

There are countless ways we can introduce others into this wonder-filled Kingdom, helping them experience the outpouring from an Open Heaven into a thirsty, hungry earth. Whether it is leading thousands in huge gatherings in stadiums like some of my friends do; in smaller conferences and meetings; in one-on-one in the streets, shops, cafés and restaurants; or through building intimate relationships, God is releasing us all into this honor of introducing others into His world. It's like leading someone to the waterfall and encouraging him to stand underneath its flow, feeling the fullness of its glory pour all over him.

There's an extraordinary delight in watching someone, or many someones, come into alignment themselves with the Plumb Line of Heaven, especially for the first time. You can see them move closer, watch with joy as each one in his or her own uniqueness draws near to the glorious alignment they don't yet see, but you watch its magnetic force begin to pull them into an alignment that was fashioned just for that one, from the very beginning, by the God who loves and knows that one, who even placed gifts and callings, purpose and destiny inside. Sometimes, when I look at those "things that are unseen,"[3] I can see God's love streaming down from Heaven like a giant cylindrical beam of glorious light, pulsing and charged with electric energy. The hungry one draws near, feeling a pull but not yet knowing what will happen. As that one begins to experience God's love, he turns into it and steps inside … and then it happens. There's Jesus. Suddenly, Holy Spirit within, together with the spirit of the man, embrace Holy Spirit moving all around:

> "The Spirit Himself bears witness with our spirit that we are children of God, and if children, then heirs—heirs of God and joint heirs with Christ …"
>
> —PAUL[4]

That one is suddenly in the center of that portal of light and energy and power, under that waterfall of Heaven pouring into the earth, in alignment with the Plumb Line, and then he experiences promise and purpose and destiny and that great, great love of God pouring into and over and all around him, and he's forever changed and sealed and wrecked by Heaven, and nothing else can ever satisfy. It's the new creation, and it's what we are created for.

Each summer, we take a group of young princes sailing in the Caribbean to introduce them to life in the Spirit. For nine days, we live in metaphor, led by the Spirit in dreams, coincidences, prophesies, revelations, scripture, wisdom; phenomena in nature, weather, wind and water; and by navigation, sail, and rudder. On the second night at sea, one by one, they confess their fears and break agreement with them, then step off the aft deck into impossibility to walk on water. Striving and performance are broken off their lives as we celebrate the sheer act of stepping out in faith; then as they encounter God, miracles break out. Freedom, healing, prophecy, joy, and outpourings of the Holy Spirit erupt. A new generation of Water Walkers emerge.

DIVINE APPOINTMENT: THE ADVENTURE BEGINS

A young man asked if he could meet with me. He was a second-year student at Bethel School of Supernatural Ministry, and he was considering internship for his third year, exploring me as a mentor. Since he'd served in the Healing Rooms for two years, I knew him somewhat and enjoyed his enthusiasm. Yet there was a slight awkwardness as he wrestled with what he felt God was telling him to say to me.

Tell him you have a boat, Holy Spirit prompted him.

"I feel like I'm supposed to tell you I have a sailboat," he said. Pause. "It's a fifty-two-foot catamaran in the British Virgin Islands."

I was visibly impacted as he told me that he and his brother had been leading trips for ten years, taking young men on adventures into discovery on the open seas while teaching them to sail. He couldn't have known; only God knew. As I looked at him, astounded, he replied, "What?"

"Thirty years ago, I wrote on my 'Dream List' that I wanted to teach a revival school on a sailboat in the Caribbean. It's one of those impossible dreams because I have no access to a boat, only minimal sailing skills from my boyhood, I don't know a captain with a boat, and I have never been past Key West into the Caribbean. It's sunk way down on the dream list to the point of almost being forgotten."

"Well, I have a captain's license, the lease of this amazing catamaran, and a group of ten young men excited to go for two weeks this summer," he said. "Want to be our revival teacher?"

My head was spinning.

And that's how I came to know Benjamin and his brother Matthew. Matt taught both Outdoor Adventure and Literature at a well-known prep school, and the brothers had led teams of students backpacking, mountaineering, rock climbing, and sailing as part of the school's winter-quarter "experience" track. But the previous year, Benjamin had attended Bethel School of Supernatural Ministry and had himself experienced mammoth encounters with Holy Spirit, prophecy, healing, signs, wonders, and miracles. So basically, Holy Spirit had hijacked last year's sailing trip, and the students returned home healed, prophesying, filled with the Spirit, hugely impacted, lives changed, and telling all sorts of tales of spiritual adventures as yet unheard of in the annals of that conservative private Christian school's experience. Bit of a shake-up …

In the shock waves that ensued, the trip for the coming year was canceled while the leadership of the school navigated some stormy waters. Matt and Ben decided to start their own company, Expedition 61 (from Isaiah 61), to begin taking trips outside the parameters of the Christian high school. The school agreed that students, after graduating and with parental permission, could voluntarily join the trip. These boys had been looking forward their entire high school careers to this climax of their senior year because they'd been regaled with the amazing tales of fun and adventure on the high seas from seniors in years gone by. A trip was coming together for July, and I was invited along.

Being from Colorado, I love hiking and climbing the peaks, and since the early 1980s had led trips into the wilderness with my buddy Jody, taking high school boys backpacking into discovery of the creation, the Creator, and themselves in the enormous playground of the Rocky Mountains. It's something that makes me come alive: encouraging and empowering young princes as they step into the realm of metaphor and Divine coincidence and begin to see everything through different lenses as Holy Spirit takes the fabulous created world of wonder around us and speaks personal truth, love, purpose, and destiny in undeniable ways that change us forever! So to do it on the sea, in the tropics, on a sailboat … I was excited, to say the least. I still marvel at how God does it, how He interweaves His dreams with ours until they seamlessly unfold as if we had planned them together. It is truly a wonder that He has listened to our boyhood dreams and the desires of our hearts and never forgets but resurrects and breathes life into them at the perfect time, in the fullness of time, at just that time when we have learned to delight ourselves in Him and He can cause us to bring forth the most fruit, while it seems like all we are doing is abiding in Him. *Oh God, I love Your ways! You are making me fall in love with You all over again.*

As a trial run in his application process for third-year internship, I took Benjamin on a one-week ministry trip to Switzerland that spring; he took me on a two-week sailing trip to the British Virgin Islands that summer of 2016. I guess we both passed the test since he interned for me during the 2016–2017 school year and we have been friends ever since.

FIRST MIRACLES

We all met as a team for the first time at O'Hare Airport in Chicago that summer of 2016, and we saw our first half-dozen miracles there. As the Redding crew stepped off the plane from San Francisco, we spotted a coffee kiosk and decided to grab a double espresso before meeting the others. My travel backpack has wonderful secret pockets, and as I went for the one that always holds my wallet, I found it unzipped and empty. Oh no! I searched throughout the pack and found no wallet, so I sprinted back to the gate, but everyone had disembarked, and they wouldn't allow me back on the plane. A flight attendant offered to go check and returned saying she'd covered the entire area, seat and seat pocket, overhead, underneath, on the floor—and found nothing.

I went back to Benjamin, and we tore through my bag and searched every pocket, unloading all the contents. Concerned for my credit cards, I texted Linda to be ready to call the companies and cancel if we didn't find them. I looked at Benjamin, and we declared together: "I want my wallet back!" Then I opened my re-packed backpack one more time, and there, sitting in plain view directly on top, was my wallet! *How did You do that, Lord?*

Getting fourteen guys and eighteen bags of gear and equipment through baggage check and within proper weight was a miracle itself. We received unprecedented favor with one airline official who prioritized our luggage through to the final destination without having to collect and re-check it, contrary to the airline's procedure. Several bags needed to be rearranged and consolidated, however, and in the melee that ensued, our chief engineer Leigh threw some of his gear into his carry-on to save weight. When he went through the security scanner, his twelve-inch diving knife had made it into his backpack! The TSA officials could only laugh as it showed up on their screen. Fortuitously, as he ran back to baggage check with the blade in hand, the last of our bags had not yet left on the conveyor belt, and he was able to cache it.

While in the airport as we were tackling difficulties, Matthew became suddenly very ill. He couldn't stand or walk, was overcome by chills and sweat, and had trouble breathing; we found him a wheelchair and pushed him to a quiet place while the team went about finding food and attending to other needs. He was in a state where he could not board a plane and was being attacked by judgment, fear, and accusation. He was supposed to be a leader of this "supernatural adventure," and he was suddenly helpless, weak, and defeated. We all prayed for him, and, finally, several of us stayed and ministered to him.

I saw that he was assaulted with slander and injustice; the weight of all the accusations and attacks from the previous trip and its repercussions were heavy upon him. He languished for over an hour under this pall, and then suddenly, the prayers were answered and as quickly as the attack had hit, it suddenly departed. He was up, peace came, and with it quiet victory!

Life on a boat with fourteen men is an adventure at many levels, and building community and family is one of the greatest joys. Being in a limited space with limited provisions is an awesome opportunity to see wonders! We became teams to prepare meals, and as one of the students and I prepared our breakfast of eggs scrambled with delightful things inside, we had a specific ration of food to work with. But as we cooked and served, the pans got more full, and we kept cooking, and instead of decrease, there was increase. The more we served, the more there was! It wasn't need that orchestrated the multiplication of the food but simply the delight of God to show us wonders and illustrate the abundance of Heaven He was inviting us into.

We had a desalinator on board that turned seawater into fresh—a wonderful miracle of technology! It took about five hours to fill both tanks, and we had to check them regularly, wanting to operate the system at night when we weren't sailing. Living at sea and not desiring to return to port, we used a lot of water. One morning, Benjamin noticed the desalinator had stopped functioning, and he and first mate Leigh and our mechanic Josiah worked on it with no success. Early the next morning, one tank was empty and the other at about ten percent, so Benjamin tried three times to reboot it. We stopped to have our morning coffee and decided to celebrate instead of frustrate.

We began thanking God for everything: the fish swimming around the boat in the clear aqua water, the gorgeous sunrise, the boat with its mast and sails, and everything that caught our eyes as we looked around. As we rejoiced, we began to declare wholeness to the desalinator and continued to declare healing over it. Benjamin went over and hit the button, and it kicked on! We celebrated some more!

Figuring we'd have to stay at anchorage for about five hours, we got busy with other things until some of the guys who were swimming around the boat shouted that water was gushing out of the overflow from the tanks. What normally took five hours to fill suddenly filled in forty-five minutes as the water multiplied in the tanks, making up for a day of dysfunction. *You always cause us to wonder, Lord!*

We also saw wonders in the natural world around us. As we all jumped off the deck into the warm Caribbean waters to swim and frolic, Benjamin realized he'd had his expensive sailing sunglasses on his head as he plunged into the water. They were a gift from his wife, and they quickly disappeared beneath the sea. The aqua blue water was so clear you could see the bottom, eighteen feet below, and we all joined him as he searched for any sign of them, scanning the depths. We prayed, and he called out for God's help. Just then, a giant manta ray with a ten-foot tail glided across the bottom and stopped below us. It was gorgeous, with circles of silvery gold on its back that caught the sunlight, even beneath the sea. We marveled at its beauty and then watched it swim away.

Again we searched, and Benjamin asked God for help. The manta ray returned and stopped in the same spot at the bottom of the sea. Again we marveled at its glory, and again it swam away. One of our young men was a deep diver and explored a few shiny reflections we spotted but to no avail. Ben called out to God, and for a third time, the manta ray returned and stopped in the same place, causing us to greatly wonder. When it left, there were Benjamin's sunglasses, sitting on a conch shell directly under the place where the ray had hovered. Our diver swam to the bottom and brought them up, and we all celebrated the goodness of God and delighted in His assistance, especially recognizing how He uses all of creation to display His love and glory! There are no limits to the extent of His ability to connect with us, and we've found that coincidences and repetition are some of the ways He loves to use.

WALKING ON WATER

We taught these amazing and powerful young men about a relationship with Holy Spirit that defies all limitation and rational boundaries: a supernatural reality that lives both within and beyond the borders of the conservative religious culture they were accustomed to. All possibility opened up, and we asked them to come into the middle of the group and be seated on the chair, one by one, as each was ready to take the challenge to step off the boat and walk across the water to Jesus. The second year we did this, I asked each young man to speak out the things he feared, to declare them and bring them into the open where truth can demolish them. It was remarkable to me that every young man confessed fears of not being enough, not measuring up, of being rejected for unacceptable and unimpressive performance and failure. Many of these are the sons of high-profile achievers in many realms, educated for greatness in the best schools. And yet that fear of failure pervaded.

We took these fears and flushed them down a prophetic toilet. We prophesied over each one in turn, then blessed him and watched him walk down the aft stairs, look right into Jesus—and, when ready, step out onto the glassy sea and walk to Him. The tropical night was pregnant with expectation and excitement. One by one, each young man stepped off the aft deck and … *Splash!* Straight into and under the great blue sea.

But three things happened that night.

First, each man faced impossibility, and rejecting fear of failure, with joy and trepidation, stepped right into it!

Second, each one emerged to the cheers and praises of all his mates, who applauded him and then hugged and congratulated him as they helped him back on board. These young men had never been celebrated for "failure" before. It demolished that suffocating spirit of performance!

And third, each one had an encounter with God in and under the water. Some saw visions, others heard words of destiny or affirmation, one had what he felt was an hour-long encounter with Jesus underwater while we saw him submerged for only moments. All felt His great love, pleasure, and acceptance. Something happened that broke off the religious demands of striving and working for approval. There's always a lie that tries to get us to work for something that's already been freely given. That night, a group of men came into the glorious freedom of the children of God.

Under the magnificent tropical full moon, we all ended the night by diving into the warm Caribbean waters and delighting in the wonder of God's love and creation. As we frolicked in the moonlit sea, we were encompassed by swarms of glowing, bioluminescent algae. It was as if the stars came down to kiss the sea and embrace us with sparkling delight! All creation declares His glory.

SAILING JOURNAL, JULY 2017

There's something raw and fresh and beautiful about journal entries written while still under the influence of the adventure, poems written in the afterglow of wonder, as the mind slows down to reflect and the emotions are still reverberating from the experience. After a full wild day of wind, sea, and sun, we'll anchor in a protected bay where the wind turns into the gentlest breeze and the water becomes calm and glassy. While the crew makes dinner in the galley, I'll sit on the foredeck in the shade of the flybridge, back toward the evening sun, tablet in my lap, connecting with Holy Spirit as I recall and thank Him for the joys of the day. The galley window opens, and my wild-haired Italian friend pops his head out to bless me with a cup of freshly made espresso with hot foamed cream, which I sip as I type on the keypad as the memories roll and the emotions return. It's a rare quiet space on a ship of fourteen men, and I glory in the fellowship of the Holy Spirit as we write together in the midst of this tropical paradise.

Night Crossing to St. Bart's, 7/16/17: We hoisted our sails into the dark, open sea, into a powerful head wind with the huge swelling roll of the great deep splashing over the bow, sailing south, directly into nine-foot waves as we howled with joy in the full spray. Half-moon smiled on us in the blackness, Africa way off to port side, Belize somewhere to starboard, a whole world of wide open sea. Men in harnesses leashed to the lifelines moved along the rolling decks of the fifty-two-foot catamaran. We sailed for three hours from night into the soft pink of dawn until the yellow orb of the sun, framed in cumulus clouds, broke the horizon. And then we sailed on, past rocky island mountains until we reached the gorgeous harbor of Gustavia with its huge rock sentinels and crystal clear, impossibly blue water: such a blue that one can't stop marveling, whether swimming in it or looking down to the fish and sea turtles below. A Safe Harbor.

A Dream in the Night, 7/17/17: We were anchored in the rocky embrace of the Île Fourchue, a tiny uninhabited island in the Lesser Antilles whose mountain slid down into rocky cliff arms that formed a protected bay, filled with coral and tropical fish. After a day of snorkeling and a night of feasting and activating young men to prophesy, I awoke, lifting my head from my pillow on the aft deck to survey a glorious dawn over an aqua blue sea. The early riser, I started first coffee as I puzzled over the curious dream still fresh in my head. Taking my coffee up to the fly deck is a bit of a dance with the sway of the boat and the spiral stairs and the scalding hot cup full of glory and goodness, but way easier than under full sail. Benjamin joined me on the comfy couch at the helm as we viewed the splendor of the Caribbean morning—with coffee. I told him my dream.

It was a simple dream but one that left me thinking I'd just been told a secret I didn't fully understand. I told Benjamin: "You and I were outside a huge brick school building trying to enter by the side door, but when we tried it, we found the outer door broken and had to force it. Inside the vestibule, the inner door had been completely bricked over so there was no entry. We had to go around to the front door, which was in perfect condition and afforded us easy entrance."

"I know what it means!" exclaimed Benjamin. We had been discussing sailing west this morning to a tall volcanic mountain island to explore and snorkel and later sail north to Anguilla.

"The North, or leeward entry, is known as the 'Front Door.' To explore the western island would be the 'side door,' which apparently is closed to us."

Storm warnings were in effect, and other small ships had left this tiny bay in the evening or very early this morning. We took it as a word to head north now and make the four-hour crossing before the storm. We later learned that the tall volcano had no anchorage, dropping abruptly into deep sea, affording "no entry." Thank You for Your guidance, Lord. We've been "schooled!"

Passage to Anguilla, 7/17/17: Under full sail, we headed north with a strong wind, traveling at nine knots in a heaving open sea for a four-hour crossing. Arriving at the gates through the islands, we checked the time, and only two hours had passed ... No one knows what happened to those other two hours.

The Knighting, Scrub Island, 7/17/17: On the evening of the sixth day, we sailed to a pristine beach on a deserted island to celebrate their passage and growth in learning, prophesying, outreach, healing, sailing, miracles, snorkeling, service, anointing, fun, and rejecting lies and embracing truth. Each prince got alone with God until he heard God's heart for him and discovered his God-given identity and took on a new name, writing out and then declaring to all of us what God had shown him of his destiny, purpose, and then the commitments he would make to get there. On that beach, under an Open Heaven, before God and their brothers, I knighted them one by one, each with his new name. Afterward, there was the greatest eruption of Holy Spirit freedom, love, and joy we have yet experienced!

It was as if the Holy Spirit tossed a hand grenade into the midst of us. Young men flew backward into the soft white sand, then staggered like drunken sailors as they wrestled, dogpiled, and rolled about on the beach, laughing ecstatically and reeling in uninhibited freedom and joy. Exhilaration erupted into leaping, dancing, and tackling each other as sunset faded into twilight.

We had to make two trips in the dinghy from beach to ship to all get aboard. I went in the first shift as I was on dinner duty, but that left seven of the most wildly drunk in the Holy Spirit young men alone on the beach for about a half hour. Most of them had never experienced this aspect of Holy Spirit: the fun, wild, gloriously uninhibited freedom that unlocks and heals deep places of control and pain that have been stuffed for years. Sometimes the physical body can't respond to such explosive freedom and healing, and the ability to walk or even crawl is compromised. It's a control freak's nightmare, but in reality his best friend! It's called freedom, and doesn't look pretty or composed; often more like a train wreck. However, we've seen so many times the fruit of just one encounter where Holy Spirit pushes all your buttons at once and fries your circuits. Pride, arrogance, control, denial, buried rejection, and pain are all blown out, and what is left is a beautiful humility, a revelation of God's love for you and the "glorious freedom of the children of God."[5] So we rejoiced with the lads.

Josiah took the dinghy back to the beach and helped throw bodies over the inflated sides, but the challenge was to keep them all in as they motored across the sea. From my place in the galley, I heard the commotion of their arrival. I was myself pretty wrecked on Holy Spirit joy, but I have years of practice at functioning while under the influence. We call it "drunktional." I was standing at the chopping block with two huge kitchen knives in my hands, looking over a pile of vegetables and shrimp and asking Holy Spirit for a strategy while I seemed to repeat over and over, "OK, what am I doing?" while I swung about two deadly blades in my hands as the ship gently swayed. My cooking helper was useless in his present state, so I dismissed him to play with the others in the aft lounge. Every now and again, an explosion of laughing, reeling boys would come at me in the galley, and I would turn, wave the knives at them, and shout: "Out! I have deadly weapons!" By some amazing miracle, and Leigh's help, we pulled it off, and the meal was outstanding, served as the boys were coming down a bit and feeling ravenously hungry.

Across Anguilla, 7/18/17: We took off in the morning with gale-force tailwinds of 30 mph and followed the north shore of Anguilla, traveling west at a speed of about fourteen knots under only our jib while we surfed the nine-foot waves on a fifty-two-foot "surfboard" for half an hour! Dolphins joined us for the fun as they played and leapt like guardians alongside our double bow. Sheer delight!

BAND OF BROTHERS

One of my greatest joys comes from seeing someone get it. Suddenly, there's a spark, and something is ignited within that changes the scope of everything, how you see and think and process. A lens is replaced, and all at once, you see it all through Love! This happened on the boat one night in such a remarkable way. It was toward the end of the cruise in 2018, and all the guys wanted to have a night of worship. I suggested they pass the guitar around, as each has their own unique style. I watched as they began to "own it," to take charge and go where the Spirit was leading. We were on the aft deck in the starlight, and we leaders drifted into the background and observed. Ben, Matt, and Josiah actually moved into the galley to talk over things, and I leaned back against the cushion by my cabin door and delighted in hearing their hearts as they sang songs and strummed guitar riffs, interspersed with revelations they were having. One young man had cut his foot that day and was in pain. Suddenly, another said: "It's not right for Cody to be in pain and not be healed! Can we pray for him?" The question was directed toward me, and I backed off, saying, "You guys have got it. Go for it!" They prayed several times and saw a tiny reduction in pain, but they were not satisfied.

"What do we do now, Chuck?"

"What *do* we do now, guys?" I responded. We'd had teaching in the previous days on healing and connecting with God.

"Oh yeah, we ask God what He's doing and saying!" one of our all-stars replied.

They asked. I'd heard moments before that they were to love him, that he was becoming a project, and that it was time to stop trying and simply love him, but I didn't say a word as I wanted them to hear from God.

"I think we're supposed to gather around Cody and love him. Just pour out God's love and our love all over him," interjected another.

They brought him into the middle and began praying and then pressing in and hugging, embracing him. Tears began to flow. They prophesied and encouraged him, spoke words of value and life and hope and affirmation over him. Cody had been through a lot of hardship, pain, and rejection that year, and it was a miracle that he'd even made it on the trip. This outpouring of love from these men went deeper than we even knew, canceled assignments from the enemy to destroy him, and brought him more firmly into Life and life more abundantly.

Benjamin stepped through the galley door, beaming with pride and joy as he caught my eye, and we watched these young princes become family, a band of brothers fully engaged and occupied with one brother's pain. My heart welled up in my chest, and my eyes filled with moisture. Cody's pain diminished, and he began to see increased movement in his toes. But the even greater work became established in his heart. We all cheered and praised and thanked Jesus! But my overwhelming joy came from seeing a group of disparate boys become family, one, "His body, the fullness of Him who fills everything in every way ..."[6] and the manifold wisdom of God made known to the rulers and authorities in the heavenly places,[7] living stones being built into a spiritual house, built together into a dwelling place of God in the Spirit:[8] His Church.

THE BITTER END YACHT CLUB

After a week at sea, living in board shorts, sailing, swimming, and snorkeling, hair full of salt water, wind, and sand, we cleaned up nicely, put on fresh clothes and our best flip-flops, and moored in the harbor of the Bitter End Yacht Club. We'd planned a dinner celebration for the West Indian Barbecue buffet at the upscale resort and had a table for fourteen reserved. Fourteen hungry men eyed the huge spread.

As our waitress served us drinks, I sensed she had pain in her elbow, and I questioned her about it as I asked her name. It was a setup.

"Oh yes, I do! But the pain in my back is worse," she declared.

"These young men would like to pray for you if that's OK."

They looked a little surprised, but with a thirty-second prayer, all the pain left her body. She was ecstatic! As she headed to the kitchen checking out her new, pain-free body, the guys were overjoyed. One of our young men who'd previously been plagued by fear spoke up. He had taken on the new name "Nathaniel the Fearless."

"I had a prophetic word for her, but I was too chicken to give it."

"Yolanda!" I shouted out to her just before she got to the kitchen door. "This young man has a word for you."

She returned to our table with expectant, sparkling eyes to find out what Nate had to tell her. He prophesied beautifully, and she cried at God's love and tenderness toward her. Nathaniel beamed. I decided to take it further.

"Nate, you see that table over there with the young couple who look about nineteen years old? I think they're newlyweds, and I want you to go over to them and give them a prophetic word and pray for their marriage."

"Okay!" And he took a deep breath and headed for their table while we watched from the distance. Smiles, words, prayer, tears, hugs ... Nate was stellar.

Aiden stood up and said, "That group over at the big table intimidates me; they're all so athletic, good-looking, professional, wealthy. I'm going to go and prophesy over them!" And he headed for a table of young couples just as Nate returned.

"I'll go with you," Nathaniel exclaimed. We watched those boys shine and rejoiced.

Yolanda returned to our table with a friend from the kitchen who also needed healing. And then another. Then the manager brought out a woman who needed healing but also didn't know Jesus. As she received His love for the first time, we all celebrated. More staff members came to our table throughout the night for healing, and that Healer kept doing His thing: healing all the people who came to Him!

As we continued laughing, praying, prophesying, eating and drinking, celebrating, and generally enjoying the night, two women walked past our table to be seated nearby. I asked them how they were doing, and one responded, "Oh, I'm making it." I looked at our boys and knew that four of them were amazing singers, so I asked the two women if they would mind if these young men sang over them at their table. A little surprised, the women nodded, and the boys stood around them. Then, in wonderful four-part harmony, they proceeded to sing a beautiful chorus over them. The women wept. More hugging, praying, prophesying.

Another West Indian employee sat in her white uniform in the midst of a group of our guys at the far end of the table, and they prayed with her for her wayward son. Love, joy, hope, and community broke out throughout the yacht club that night as revival flowed from our team in a way they had never experienced before. Our boys were elated!

"Have you ever seen anything like this before?" they asked.

"This is your new normal, guys!" I told them.

CURRENTS IN THE SKY AND SEA

Our days are spent buoyant,
a little world afloat
in that curious space between the sea and sky.

Strong currents are like mighty rivers
flowing through the deep
that seem to scatter upon the surface
with the blast of every breeze.

The mighty wind forms currents
blowing through the atmosphere,
and yet that powerful breath
responds to every moving thing that passes through.

All day we ride the heave and swell and spray
of the great blue waves,
moved by those winds, trimmed by these sails.
And afterward we anchor in a place
the rocky land embraces.
The mighty currents are diverted for the night,
and we find rest.

That's when the magic of a glorious sky,
deep blackness pulsing with galaxies above,
dropping meteor showers on every side,
then blends and interweaves
with the magic of lights swimming in the sea:
the marvels of constellations twinkling and stars shooting up
above
meet bioluminescent algae sparkling and exploding down
below.

In between we ride them both
14 men on a grand adventure,
riding the currents of this natural realm;
learning the currents of His Holy Spirit,
sailing into wonder.
10 young men
will never be the same.

IT'S ALL ABOUT
THE WONDER

"Learn this well:
Unless you dramatically change your way of thinking
and become teachable, and learn about heaven's kingdom realm
with the wide-eyed wonder of a child,
you will never be able to enter in."

—JESUS[1]

AN EARLY SAILING ADVENTURE, SPRING 1966
At the age of sixteen, I won our school sailing regatta. It was actually something of a fluke; I wasn't a great sailor and was on the verge of being kicked out of that elite private boarding school. But in spite of being unfavored and unapproved, it happened: I won. I've often remembered it with a certain humorous irony, which completely unraveled this past year as God began to show me where He was in all of it. Wow. Now it overwhelms and truly humbles me.

I'd recently been drawn to watch a 1989 flick called *Dead Poets Society* that happened to be filmed on the campus of the boys' boarding school I attended in my freshman and sophomore years. Memories flooded back with all the varied emotions and intrigue that accompanied that era. I had no personal knowledge of God or Jesus at that time and didn't even know there was a Holy Spirit. It was a confusing and troubling span of life.

I'd grown up in a large family: I have forty-eight first cousins! My mother was one of seven siblings and my father one of seven brothers. It was a large, very caring family, and I grew up knowing I was valued and loved, empowered to believe I could be anything I wanted. In my experience, it was more on the grace-filled end of the spectrum than the tyrannical.

Then I went to boarding school. Now that was The Law! Everywhere were rules and regulations: everything you couldn't do, couldn't enjoy, and couldn't have. Plus heaps of competition. I reacted to it as a challenge, taking it on as a game with a bit of mischief and delight. (I'm not implying that was the correct response; it's just the path I chose.)

In my first month as a student, I received more demerits than any other student in the history of the school. Thirty-five years later, I reconnected with an old schoolmate from that era.

"You were something of a folk hero," he told me.

"Really? How's that?" I asked.

"You were the one who did everything we ever wanted to but were afraid to do."

"Yeah, and you graduated, and I'm the one who was expelled!" I replied as we laughed about it.

In the film, there is a group of naughty boys with whom I easily identified; the memories flooded in, much more full of raw emotion and detail than I expected. And I really wasn't expecting the encounter with God that happened shortly thereafter. He began to show me how much He was involved in my life at that time and how He was moving prophetically even then to highlight the future He had for me just as soon as I was willing and able to turn toward Him.

I was rather popular and really liked the group of friends I had. Because of my bad choices, the administration began to speak to the other lads, both individually and corporately, warning them to stay away from me—in fact, to have nothing to do with me. I was nominated for a class office, and a meeting was convened in which the other students were told my name must be taken off the list while I was told to stay in my room and not attend the meeting. As you can imagine, there was a sense of betrayal and injustice I felt at all this. There was no place the leaders of the school wanted to see me highlighted.

This is the backdrop to the story as God began to walk with me through this confusing time to show me where He was and how much He loved me, even in my rebellion.

The school sailing regatta took place in the springtime on the beautiful lake the academy overlooked. I was paired with another lad; we crewed a small, single-sailed Penguin. As all the boats gathered, hoisting mainsails for the race, the bow of our small craft crossed the starting line just before the horn sounded. The others bolted toward the south to catch the favored starboard tack as the wind blew directly toward us from the buoy at the east end of the lake, which was our turning point. To avoid disqualification I needed to come about and re-cross the starting line to enter the race. Well behind the others now as we looped around, we took off to the north, taking the least favored port tack across the lake with not another boat before us on our route.

We headed out with glee as if in our own race, rejoicing at the wind in our sails and looking with wonder at the sky above and rippling water beneath. To the crowd on the shore, we looked more like the village idiots. But something about our situation filled us with joy as we chose not to look at failure, instead working with sail and rudder, exploring that subtle relationship between the two that releases the utmost momentum, and feeling how the currents in the wind and water played upon our little boat. We laughed together, purposing to make it to the buoy and back while delighting in the magic of a ship under sail, ripping across the surface of the lake, powered by the very wind itself. Something of the wonder of *Now*, living fully in that moment, overtook us, and we were filled with a joy that had nothing to do with our position in the fleet or in the race but everything to do with being fully alive and in motion right now!

More than halfway across the lake, the other boats were beginning their tack toward the buoy. We marveled as suddenly we saw the wind actually shift and begin to blow from the northeast, directly into the whole fleet, but greatly in our favor as we switched tack, with a strong wind coming at our port side, speeding us toward the buoy. We sliced around it and began our homeward journey under full sail, now in the favored position and ahead of all the others who were trying to beat into the wind to round the buoy. We won the race—greatly to the embarrassment of the authorities, who did not want me celebrated.

I've occasionally remembered the unique irony of that story, but as God began to speak to me about it, He showed me something wonderful! He said He loved to watch me doing life, and what He saw was portrayed in that regatta. Many times, in many situations, I'd been disqualified, sometimes by my own poor choices and sometimes simply by the circumstances of life. But He always took pleasure and cheered me on as I got back up and faced the situation with wonder and delight. It was my sense of wonder that He loved!

In a sudden revelation of His heart and plans, I saw that He had in fact placed that sense of wonder in me; He'd planted it as a precious seed, and His delight in me was in how I played with it and nurtured it! He showed me how that race was a prophetic sequence for my whole life. I'd head toward goals, like that buoy, yet in the race toward it, never lose sight of the wonder all around. And as I kept my attention open to the wonder, He changed the wind!

God told me that He'd done it many times since then, and even thinking about it, I can see the movies play out, reliving many varied experiences where I could see the end, much like the buoy, but faced some overwhelming odds and even impossibilities along the way.

I now watched from God's perspective as I'd search about me; rather than fix my attention on the limitations of the problem, I'd observe the magic all around. There's always wonder to be found! And each time I'd look into the wonder of unlimited possibility, a metaphoric wind would shift, and something miraculous would happen, although to some it looked coincidental. He showed me how easily we can be tricked and trapped by the goal and by the competitive focus to reach that goal, take the prize, and even do it with the best form, according to all the rules, yet miss the wonder He's placed right before us. That wonder can be as subtle as the still, small voice or the gentle nudge of His Spirit as we're charging ahead in the work of the Kingdom. We can be caught up in religious zeal and miss the magic of the relationship He has for us on the journey, which is the true prize.

Here I am at seventy years, and I've just caught on how consistently He's been playing like that with me since my teens, since before I knew He was my Father, before I knew He loved and championed me and had such plans for me. He accepted me before I ever asked Him to. Always He's been my biggest fan, cheering me on. And now in this season of my life, He's wanting to take me into stories from the distant past just to show me how far back and unconditional was His love for me, how intentional and consistently pursuing He has always been toward me. Never did He condemn or reject me for all of those poor choices, never rail or berate me or withdraw His affections or promises, His gifts, and His callings. They were always there before I even knew Him, waiting for me to fully engage in the game, always available for me to use well or even misuse while He patiently wooed me and planted seeds of divine encounter in front of me until they began to spring up and attract my attention, drawing me into a pursuit I thought I was initiating.

"Drip down, O heavens, from above,
And let the clouds pour down righteousness;
Let the earth open up and salvation bear fruit,
And righteousness spring up with it.
I, the LORD, have created it."

—GOD[2]

Oh God, You are a wonder, a relentless lover, a wonderful counselor, mighty God, everlasting Father, Prince of Peace … of the increase of Your government and peace there will be no end.[3] Thank You for Your government of love and empowerment that defies punishment, Your mercy and loving kindness that triumph over judgment[4] throughout all the eras of my life!

THE WONDERS OF HIS LOVE

As we interact with His word, which is Truth, and His Holy Spirit, who is the Spirit of Truth, we might still be deceived and corrupted into thinking that we have to come into alignment with some standard of conformity, some persona that is acceptable to some unknown committee that affirms whether we are, in fact, really valid followers of Jesus. The true wonder of His love and grace is that He loves diversity, and as Creator, He has produced an unlimited array of diverse beauty and creativity. Earlier, we studied the meaning of the word *abide* and found that it means "to remain, stay, be present, be here now …" It also means to remain *me* here now, resisting every temptation to compare ourselves with others or strive to be like another, but to be truly *ourselves*, present with Him, here now, uniquely and uncompromisingly ourselves in the presence of God. You have permission to be *you*! It's wonderful!

As God took me through different eras of my life recently, He showed me how much He loved and affirmed the unique person I am, never comparing me to another. He has never seen me as a short-fall when standing next to some giant but always affirmed as beautiful and unparalleled, "fearfully and wonderfully made." He planned *me*. And the best way I can bring Him glory is to be fully *me*. There is a *life message* that I alone carry that is me—more than the message I teach, but the very source from which it flows, a letter written in the heart, known and read by all … a letter from Christ, written not with ink but with the Spirit of the living God. As I give myself permission to be fully me and live out that letter from the heart of God, I find that He has written in every era of my life, and nothing of His plans and purposes is wasted.

Each letter is unique. You are a life message, and there is no other like you. I'm not talking about our toxic self-absorption but the deeper gifts and callings that stir within, motivating us to pursue the adventure of life, each in our own unique way. It's our unique interaction with His truth, in the Word and the Spirit, that sets us apart for greatness. His word is like the map, and His Spirit is the heavenly GPS. Through all the eras of our lives He's been there. With every choice to reject the map and launch out on our own and become miserably lost, His precious voice says: *"Recalibrating,"* and He shows us the new route to get us into our destiny. It's wondrous!

SAILING INTO WONDER, SUMMER 2018

Before the sailing trip in July 2018, we held a conference so the students and their parents could catch a glimpse of what we'd be learning and experiencing on the boat and so they'd be trained to host, interact with, and steward God's supernatural presence and power in our midst—those wonderful gifts freely given to benefit any situation. Many who were hungry to experience God attended, as well as past students, and marvelous healings occurred!

I was surprised to meet the father of a young man who had come on the boat the previous year. This son was quiet and serious but had experienced the most dramatic deliverance from a stifling pressure to perform and had come into such freedom that his whole being was delirious with Holy Spirit drunkenness the evening we had our knighting ceremony. He was wrecked! For most of the trip, he slept or just hung out, things he had never been able to indulge in before. It seemed that years of high-pressure striving and performance were being washed from his whole body, soul, and spirit, and he was wallowing in glorious rest.

When I met his father, I was struck by the sobriety and seriousness of the man and somewhat surprised that he was attending. Yet his son still exuded a freedom and joy that had not diminished, only grown over the past year since our trip. He had a sister in the school who had watched him live out this transformation since returning home and hungered for it herself. She was an athlete and a runner, but for the past four years had experienced a strange condition in her hips and knees that became so severe she could not do any sports and was in constant pain. They had taken her to the best medical facilities and could not find the source of her pain, which brought on even more frustration. Everyone knew her and her situation. In one of our healing sessions at the conference, she began to weep because all the pain suddenly left her body. There was quite a commotion around her, and then she abruptly left the building to run out onto the adjoining track and sprint around it! Her father and brother went after her, dumbfounded by what was happening. When they returned, the son was rejoicing, the father wept, and his daughter shared the testimony of her complete and instantaneous healing!

Another young man brought his grandmother, who had attended the conference the previous year. She had been diagnosed with cancer and needed treatment; we had prayed for her but didn't know the outcome. She was well known in this community and asked to share, telling the whole assembly that she had gone back to her doctor and found that she no longer had any cancer in her body!

In another story from the previous year, a woman came to the conference in a wheelchair with multiple sclerosis. I had coached the people to pray very short prayers, listening to Holy Spirit for any ideas He might inspire and then acting on them. A man on the small team who prayed for her was frustrated because a woman in that group was praying a very long, religious prayer which went on and on. He was aware that I had told them to pray short prayers and then have the person do something to discover what healing had occurred. He kept waiting to interrupt the long-winded pray-er, as he had a sense that there was pain in the woman's back and something like a huge comb was sticking out that needed to be removed. At last I told them all to stop and return to their seats, at which time, the woman finally ceased praying, and the man decided to take his opportunity, asking the woman in the wheelchair if she had pain in her back. She confirmed it and he described the invisible comb and asked if they could all pull it out. She agreed and a group of them dramatically pulled until it was removed. The woman cried out that all the pain was gone! This man was studying for his Masters at the College, taking a class on Comparative Denominations, so he decided to attend our conference, which was on the charismatic end of the Christian spectrum. Afterward, he told his fellow college students about his experience in the conference and about the woman with MS. Later that summer, he was at a restaurant with these same fellow students, and a woman came up to introduce herself to him. She was the same woman in the wheelchair, and she was now walking and free from all pain! *O Jesus, thank You for healing her. Your love knows no limits!*

In the conservative Christian environment in which these young men grew up, there were some opponents to our rather radical pursuit of the miraculous and supernatural realm of the Kingdom of Heaven. Many believed that miracles had ceased with the completion of the written Bible. It was delightful to see precious people who had been wracked with pain and sickness, some for many years, be instantly healed as their families watched in awe and even wept for joy. We saw many people won over by the goodness of God displayed through His healing virtue and compassion.

The conference also gave us a chance to get to know that year's boys and their parents; the guys were a great help with all the set-up and tear-down of the event. Many of them were outgoing, bright, and cheerful, introducing themselves to me with a wholesome enthusiasm, excited for the adventure we were about to experience together.

Interestingly, the theme that kept recurring was Wonder! One of the boys kept hearing that word, as if God were speaking it to him. Before us lay an adventure, and God was leading us into wondrous encounters and countless opportunities to marvel at His goodness with awe and wonder. There was a challenge from God to stay attentive and keep looking for the wonder! I noticed among the students one young man with long, unkempt hair, glasses, and a billed cap with its straight brim pulled low, partially hiding his face. He was serving with the other boys but seemed particularly quiet, elusive, different, as if trying to fly under the radar, and he barely engaged with me at all.

THE WONDER OF GOD'S WAYS

We boarded the flight to St. Thomas, Virgin Islands, as a group and moved into a block of seats toward the rear of the plane. As I found my place, I saw that Matthew was taking the seat next to me.

"I know and love you, Matt, so I'd like to sit by one of these guys and get to know him," I said.

He agreed and got up, and I looked around, spying the kid with the long hair and the cap. I'd heard him called Cooper.

"I want to sit by you," I said as I looked him in the eye, motioning to the seat beside me. I'm not sure if it was astonishment, joy, or terror that crossed his face, but he conceded.

"So tell me, who is Cooper?" I asked as we got settled. That was the start of a conversation and friendship that didn't stop for the rest of the trip!

He was an accomplished rock climber, going to Nationals the previous year and making quite a stir, placing as a seventeen-year-old newbie. It turned out that we had a lot in common. He was something of a challenge in school, often in trouble, and had a hard time with rules. We kept comparing stories and came up with dozens of similarities. I started liking him immensely. Though he had a hard time speaking in a group, he opened up to me completely, and I heard and felt his words as he invited me in until I looked right into his heart and soul. He was an open book. Fifty years separated us, but I felt in him a kindred spirit.

I asked the question numerous times on that sailing trip: what are these feelings and why is this hitting me so deeply in my emotions, this interaction with this young man? I've discipled countless young people and seen aspects of myself in them all, felt the Father's heart for them, and guided them into encounters. This guy was a champion for sure, raw and honest and powerful, and he'd learned to protect himself from injustice with walls of defense that many can see through but few can breach. Yet he let me in so willingly.

We'd laugh and banter about our constantly discovered similarities. He'd let me call him on his stuff and later told me, "Even though you could call me on stuff, I never felt judged or condemned. I haven't really experienced that before."

And we'd tell stories. Lots of stories! I was honored by his attention and friendship; he chose me as his snorkeling partner, and we
explored the wonder of undersea palaces of coral filled with hundreds of wildly painted tropical fish of all sizes and shapes. Each
morning, he popped out of his berth to join me as I caught the dawn
easing into sunrise while I drank my organic French roast coffee and
he his yerba maté. He prioritized spending time together over his
own mates, and they honored our friendship without any ill feelings
or jealousy. I believe they really love Coop and rejoiced to see him
breaking through in ways they'd tried to help him into but without
success. Their honor and selflessness touched me deeply. His purity
of heart and lack of guile attracted me all the more to him. All of
the boys were unique, gifted, outstanding and creative, and I
enjoyed getting to know each one. I was intentional in connecting
with them as well because what was happening with Cooper was so
out in the open and obvious, above reproach, and something others
would like to experience. They all were stellar in their attitudes and
affirmations! I truly fell in love with this sensational group of young
men. But there were two areas that kept puzzling me.

For sure, I saw my younger self in him, but that has happened
many times before. This time, I was transported back in all my
memories and emotions! I felt what it was like to be eighteen, agile
and attractive, to walk into a space and have eyes fix on me; to own
the space and have others step back in awe a little. Where now I walk
into a place so I can father it and everyone in it, I used to move into
a space to confront it and sometimes call the shots, to be given place
and recognized, not completely in arrogance but surely as a challenge
and a thrill to go a little (?) over the top, to live outside the norm. I
was something of a star, but living out my unredeemed, self-focused
me—not evil or malicious, just clueless of the greater good and plan.

I saw all this and began to remember stories, thoughts, feelings,
and choices that had died with that old boy. Memories long forgotten of wild and unrighteous escapades came back so alive and

present that I questioned it all, as I knew I'd dealt with all those past attitudes, desires, and choices and that old boy was really dead. I truly am a new creation. I even remarked to Coop a dozen times at my puzzlement over this conundrum. We laughed, and he loved the crazy stories, but I was a little taken aback. I seemed to be reliving my years from sixteen to twenty-two. Very trippy and so out of the ordinary; not my best era, but definitely adventurous!

The second thing that wrenched me was the gamut of emotions I was feeling. When Cooper expressed his doubting-Thomas questions such as "Does God really care for me?" and "Since I don't hear Him, does He really want me, want to talk to me?" I felt the Father's love swell up in me so strongly that I told him God's been trying to get through to him so consistently that He finally sent me to speak it to him and to pour out love and affirmation into him. I thought it was mostly words to get Coop's attention, as it was easy for me to express that love and affirmation to this young champion. I began to feel such overwhelming love and care, to have insight into his deeper nature, and to see prophetically into his life.

It wasn't until we returned from the sailing trip and I stepped outside it, when I spent the night at Matthew's house on my way back home, that it all became clear. I sat with first coffee in the early humidity of a Midwest daybreak, in the rich lush greens of Illinois summer, tall leafy trees filtering the horizontal morning sun. I asked God: "What was that all about?"

He told me that He'd truly let me know a rather supernatural dimension of His own heart toward this young man Cooper, but in that experience, He'd taken me further. He opened up the books that live outside of time and showed me His heart for me, a young man still wild and untamed from the ages of sixteen to twenty-two. All God's pure and eternal and intimate love saw into the life of this boy, and in that, I relived some of my own drama while His love, unknown to me, was even back then pouring out all over me. That's what brought all those memories back so full of life. It was the culmination of the high school sailing regatta memory He opened to me some months before, where He began to show me where He was in those days before I ever knew Him, ever knew He knew and cared for me, planned a purpose and a life for me, carved out and engraved a destiny to shape many lives using mine in His and His in mine. It's a bit overwhelming when you think about it. Like God pulling Abraham into His own story as He calls on Abe to sacrifice his son on the very mountain where the Father would give His own Son. Then He pulls Abraham into Himself, outside of time, to reveal the wisdom of the ages, the plan and provision of God for the redemption of mankind played out in Abraham's own sacrifice—and then that miraculous provision of the ram. And Jesus explains it all in the gospels when He says, "Abraham saw My day and was glad."

I had the very great privilege of partaking of the love and the delight of the Father toward Cooper as He began to reveal His attraction, interest, delight, and love to him through me. I kind of got caught in the middle of the Plumb Line between God and him, felt the power of the current, and became a vessel for Him to speak to Cooper so he could hear. It was a bit like standing under the full force of a waterfall or in the flow of 220 volts of the Lightnings of Heaven! I'm thankful for the experience. And in the midst of it, in the timeless wonder of Heaven, I found it was the same flow that poured out on me some fifty years ago when I was clueless yet began to feel the pull I couldn't yet understand and had no frame of reference for. He loved me even then.

THE WONDER OF FULL REDEMPTION

I can now see how intricately and lovingly He was wooing me, pulling me toward Him in those days and in ways that caused me to begin to search for Him. I began to see patterns in nature and in the unseen forces I was just becoming aware of and beginning to study in those years of my life. There was a great design unfolding before me, and as the intricacies of that cosmic design in physics and in metaphysics became apparent to me, I began to devise a plan. Seeing such great design, I concurred there must be a Designer, and decided that I had to find a way to meet that overwhelmingly amazing Designer! I began to search for that One until the search became the priority and I abandoned everything else, moved to a cabin in the mountains of Colorado, and said I wouldn't leave until I'd met the Designer, the Imaginer of it all.

I thought I was the instigator, the initiator of the search … until that morning in the cabin when He showed up, when He came to me and I experienced that He is Jesus! I wasn't expecting Him, didn't know He was the One. And yet He came, introduced Himself to me, and I fell under the wild influence of His love. I found that it was He who was the initiator, the wooer. In the sailing regatta memory and in the relationship with Cooper I found the freshness of my first-love experience with Him return in all its new life and tenderness.

I believe He's always wooing us back to that: a fresh, new, vibrant, lively, bright, and vigorous relationship that never grows old or stale. This is wonder!

In this experience, I found that He daily and consistently washes us with regeneration and renewal by His Holy Spirit.[5] In each fresh encounter with Him, all of time is impacted, and our past and present, and most probably our future, are realigned. As I felt His Father love for Cooper and myself, I found that every place I'd experienced judgment, betrayal, or lack of affirmation from any friend or authority figure in my life was canceled by the unmerited love, favor, and affirmation of this astounding God who loved me past all weakness, failure, shame, rebellion, and ignorance. He had planned for me before I was, and in His great magnanimity and wisdom, love, and favor, He had decided that

I could be loved and thrive in the uniqueness of who I am, free from comparison with anyone else's standards or desires or opinions. I am free to be completely me, discovering the eternal gift of Him in me and I in Him. Every other opinion diminishes in value, and the wounds, mindsets, restrictions, and limitations placed upon me by those violations of God's love for me are washed from my spirit, soul, and body. It happens again and again through time; with each fresh revelation comes a greater experiential dimension of the glorious freedom of the children of God. He bore my wounds, and I now stand in Him, in the plumb line of Heaven, in the glorious liberty of the children of God, the assignments against my life all canceled, and I am open, wide, and free!

He showed me something else, this amazing, loving Father God. As He baptized me into the truth that He has always been for me, cheering me on, I saw the enemy's plan to discourage me exposed. Ever since those boarding-school days, I've experienced periodic waves of feeling criticized, rejected, devalued, and un-affirmed. We all experience these because that enemy is always attempting to undermine the truth that we are valued, loved, preferred, and affirmed by the Everlasting Father and highest authority in existence. If I or others look back upon that lad, we see rebellion and every sort of sin, and I found I was still slightly appalled at the remembrance of the old tales and misadventures. I'm thankful I've been made new, truly born again as that boy died! And I really marvel at that miracle in which God took all my sin and gave me His righteousness, His holiness. Wow, that is so immense and wonderful! But in the joy of that revelation, I have now recently been gutted by the fact the He, that holy God, does not look back and see the rebellion and the sin. He's not appalled. He already dealt with all my sin and guilt and shame, along with the rebellion in my heart, and died with it upon the cross a long, long time ago. All my life, He's been instead infatuated with my sense of wonder! I'm truly blown away. That is amazing grace.

Now, because I won't partner with shame for that dead past, nor will I believe the lies of rejection and criticism for being uniquely me, the enemy releases a slurry of emotions, a barrage of desire to be affirmed by someone important that I can't help but feel, that he believes are so familiar that I will embrace them as real. Yet when I look into the wonder of God's love, I find I can't embrace those desires and feelings. And through this intimate time of revelation, God showed me why:

It's the sailing regatta all over again. Because I know that boy who balked at every rule and authority is dead, and truly dead, died with Christ upon His cross and risen again with Him a new creation—because I know this to be true, even though I feel these empty, painful, familiar feelings, I can't agree and partner with them. Instead, I look around in wonder and talk to God. And now I know how much He delights in that wonder! I look into the wind and water, feel the currents that swirl around me, set my eyes upon the buoy, ply the sail and rudder—in short, play with the wonder and watch God become real. In *now* time. He's so close, He lives inside of me, He's in love with me, and I talk with Him. That alone silences all other voices, and He showed me just how much that choice defeats the enemy of our lives, aggravates and infuriates him, leaves him powerless, and pulls us into the place of immunity and freedom that has no limitations or boundaries. It's the glorious place of the wide-open spaces of the "yes" of God where He sets a banqueting table of choice delights, spreads it out before us right in the presence of our enemy, and honors us with glorious freedom.

He brought back a memory of a time in my adult life when betrayal and slander came at me from people I'd loved and invited into my heart. We were a team in ministry and worked closely together to establish God's Kingdom in the rural villages of the western Colorado mountains. Then came a rift, confusing and painful, void of loving kindness and filled with accusation and fear-filled lies that were aimed at me by those who'd been my friends. When my heart was broken and in pain, I went to them in love and encountered more rejection and judgment. I purposed to keep my heart pure and not to speak a malicious word against them, but I grieved the great loss of our love and friendship.

And then I went to Jesus, and He looked me in the eyes and said, "Oh, yes, betrayal. That one hurts so deeply. I know that one too," and He wrapped His mighty arms of love around me and pulled me in, into His own pain. With no belittling of my pain by comparing it with the immensity of His, He simply brought my heart into unity with His, one heartbeat, and my betrayal and His beat as one, and He welcomed mine to become a small piece of His gigantic, redemptive, world-changing painful betrayal. He endured all that for you and me so that we might have this Life, and more abundant Life!

As I partook of His suffering, He brought me into a greater experience of participating with Him in His glory![6] I am forever grateful.

I love you God, You lover of my soul! I know You loved me first. Let me never stop responding to the magnificent overtures of Your love for me. I want Your mighty love to explode through me like a powerful depth charge, impacting every person I come upon, that they might know that they are truly loved. Thank You from the depths of my being.

Endnotes

Introduction

[1] Romans 8:11 NKJV.
[2] John 5:19–20 NKJV.

Chapter 1: The Immediately of God

[1] Mark 1:15 TPT.
[2] James Strong, *The New Strong's Expanded Exhaustive Concordance of the Bible* (Nashville: Thomas Nelson, 2010), s.v. "immediately," Strong's Number G-2116.
[3] James Strong, *The New Strong's Expanded Exhaustive Concordance of the Bible* (Nashville: Thomas Nelson, 2010), s.v. "straightway, plumb, level," Strong's Number G-2117.
[4] John 17:22–26 NASB.
[5] Romans 6:3–8 NASB.
[6] Mark 1:4 NKJV; Luke 3:3 NKJV.
[7] John 14:12 NASB.
[8] John 14:17 NASB; Luke 24:49 NASB; Acts 1:5, 8 NASB; Acts 2:1–4 NASB.
[9] Colossians 2:14 KJV.
[10] John 17:21–23 NKJV.

Chapter 2: The Works of the Father

[1] John 5:19 TPT.
[2] John 17: 21–23, 26 TPT.
[3] John 17:17 NASB.
[4] John 8:31–32 NASB.
[5] 2 Corinthians 10:5 NKJV.
[6] John 1:14 NASB.
[7] Romans 12:2 NASB.
[8] John 14:6 NASB.
[9] John 16:13 NASB.
[10] 1 Corinthians 6:19 NASB.
[11] Haggai 2:7 NKJV.
[12] Ephesians 1:6 NKJV.
[13] John 4:23 NKJV.
[14] Romans 8:11 NASB.
[15] Psalm 72:18 NKJV.
[16] Galatians 2:20 NKJV.
[17] Galatians 2:20 TPT.
[18] Hebrews 6:18–20 TPT.

Chapter 3: The Wilderness

[1] Romans 12:2 NIV.
[2] 1 Corinthians 2:16 NKJV.
[3] John 16:13 ERV.
[4] John 16:15 NASB.
[5] Ephesians 1:13–14 NIV.

[6] Hebrews 1:2 NASB.
[7] Ephesians 1:3 NASB.
[8] Deuteronomy 8:7–9 NIV.
[9] Isaiah 64:1–2 MEV.
[10] Matthew 4:1 NASB.
[11] Matthew 6:13 NIV.
[12] 2 Corinthians 2:14 NASB.
[13] Psalm 72:18 NKJV.
[14] Romans 12:2 NIV.
[15] Exodus 14:13–14 NKJV.
[16] Romans 8:37 NKJV.
[17] Colossians 1:27 NIV.
[18] Deuteronomy 6:23 NKJV.
[19] Numbers 13:33 NKJV.
[20] Ephesians 3:10.
[21] John 14:30 NASB.
[22] Psalm 23:5.
[23] Luke 4:14 NKJV.

Chapter 4: Kingdom of Abundance

[1] Matthew 6:9–10 TPT.
[2] Luke 17:21 NKJV.
[3] John 16:13 NKJV.
[4] John 16:14–15 NIV.
[5] Titus 3:5 NKJV.
[6] 2 Corinthians 3:18 NASB.
[7] Romans 8:16 NKJV.
[8] Romans 8:11 NIV.
[9] 1 Corinthians 3:16 NKJV.
[10] Ephesians 1:23 NKJV.
[11] 1 Peter 2:5 NKJV.
[12] Ephesians 3:10 NKJV.
[13] Colossians 1:13 NKJV.
[14] 2 Corinthians 4:4–6 NASB.
[15] John 8:44 NASB.
[16] 2 Corinthians 4:4–6.
[17] Romans 10:10 NASB.
[18] Colossians 1:13 NIV; 1 Corinthians 1:30 NIV; Colossians 1:27 NIV.
[19] 1 Corinthians 1:30 NASB; Colossians 1:13 NKJV.
[20] Isaiah 9:6–7 NIV.
[21] 1 John 5:19 MEV.
[22] James Strong, *The New Strong's Expanded Exhaustive Concordance of the Bible* (Nashville: Thomas Nelson, 2010), s.v. "wickedness," Strong's Number G-4190.
[23] John 10:10 KJV.
[24] John 16:33 NASB.
[25] Romans 14:17 NKJV.
[26] James Strong, *The New Strong's Expanded Exhaustive Concordance of the Bible* (Nashville: Thomas Nelson, 2010), s.v. "saved," Strong's Number G-4982.
[27] John 10:28 NASB.

[28] Genesis 1:11.
[29] Genesis 2:15.
[30] Luke 10:18.
[31] 2 Peter 2:4.
[32] Psalm 23:5.
[33] Deuteronomy 30:19 NASB.
[34] Genesis 1:27.
[35] Genesis 2:17; John 14:6.
[36] John 17:3 NKJV.
[37] Revelation 13:8 NKJV.
[38] 1 John 3:8.
[39] John 10:10.

Chapter 5: From Having Access to Taking Possession

[1] Deuteronomy 6:23 AMPC.
[2] Joshua 5:4–7.
[3] Romans 6:11 NKJV.
[4] Romans 10:17 NASB.
[5] Matthew 11:15 NASB.
[6] 2 Corinthians 11:3 NKJV.
[7] Joshua 5:6 NKJV.
[8] Matthew 26:28 NKJV; Hebrews 8:6.
[9] Joshua 1:6, 7, 9 NASB.
[10] Joshua 1:2–7 NKJV.
[11] Joshua 3:5 NKJV.
[12] John 8:36 NASB.
[13] Galatians 5:1 NASB.
[14] John 8:32 ESV.
[15] 1 Peter 2:9 NKJV.
[16] Revelation 1:6 NKJV.
[17] 1 Corinthians 3:16–17 NASB.
[18] 1 Corinthians 6:19–20 NKJV.
[19] Ephesians 2:22 KJV.
[20] Joshua 3:15–17 NASB.
[21] Joshua 3:16 NKJV; James Strong, *The New Strong's Expanded Exhaustive Concordance of the Bible* (Nashville: Thomas Nelson, 2010), s.v. "Zaretan," Strong's Number H-6868.
[22] Romans 8:19–25 MSG.

Chapter 6: The River of God Is Full of Water

[1] Revelation 22:1 NIV.
[2] Psalm 65:9 NKJV.
[3] 1 Corinthians 2:4.
[4] Titus 3:5–6 NKJV.
[5] 1 Corinthians 4:20.
[6] Matthew 17:6; Ezekiel 1:28; Daniel 8:17.
[7] Revelation 1:17 NASB.
[8] Mark 1:10 AMPC.
[9] 2 Corinthians 4:18 NKJV.
[10] Romans 8:17.

[11] Romans 8:17.
[12] 1 Peter 1:4.
[13] Ephesians 1:13–14.
[14] John 16:14–15.
[15] John 14:12.
[16] Psalm 103:2.
[17] James 4:6.

Chapter 7: Invasions of Joy

[1] John 15:11 NKJV.
[2] Psalm 16:11 NKJV.
[3] 2 Corinthians 3:18 NKJV.
[4] John 15:11 AMP.
[5] Revelation 19:10.
[6] Exodus 15:26.
[7] Isaiah 9:3 NIV.
[8] Isaiah 65:17–18 NKJV.
[9] Revelation 12:10 NKJV.
[10] 2 Corinthians 2:14 NASB.
[11] Psalm 149:4–5 NKJV.
[12] Psalm 45:7 NLT.
[13] Psalm 5:11 NKJV.
[14] Nehemiah 8:10 NIV.
[15] Romans 8:21 NKJV.
[16] John 15:11 AMPC.
[17] Proverbs 3:5–6 NKJV.
[18] 1 John 4:4.
[19] Psalm 72:18 NKJV.
[20] Philippians 4:4 NKJV.

Chapter 8: Elevator Tales

[1] John 5:19 TPT.
[2] John 16:13–15 NIV.
[3] 2 Peter 3:9 NKJV.
[4] Romans 8:28.
[5] 2 Corinthians 12:2.
[6] 2 Corinthians 5:17 NKJV.
[7] 2 Corinthians 5:17 NKJV.
[8] John 6:63.
[9] Isaiah 53:4–5 NASB.
[10] Matthew 8:17 NASB.
[11] Romans 4:17.
[12] Psalm 23:5–6 NKJV.
[13] John 7:37–39 TPT.

Chapter 9: The Rhythm of Life

[1] Matthew 11:28–30 MSG.
[2] John 10:10 NKJV.

[3] 2 Corinthians 3:18 NKJV.
[4] Matthew 13:46.
[5] Luke 23:34 ESV.
[6] Luke 6:28.
[7] 1 John 4:19.
[8] Romans 8:11.
[9] John 16:13.
[10] Exodus 15:26 NASB.
[11] Proverbs 4:23 NASB.

Chapter 10: Building an Open-Heaven Community

[1] Daniel 11:32 NKJV.
[2] Romans 8:21.
[3] Isaiah 53:5.
[4] John 10:10.
[5] John 3:16.
[6] Revelation 22:1.
[7] Matthew 3:15.
[8] Hebrews 4:16.
[9] Matthew 10:8.
[10] Matthew 18:20 NKJV.
[11] Ephesians 4:3.
[12] Song of Songs 2:15.
[13] 1 Corinthians 3:16.
[14] Romans 8:11.
[15] Psalm 72:18 NKJV.
[16] Matthew 10:8.
[17] Ephesians 1:17.
[18] 2 Peter 1:3.
[19] Matthew 8:16–17.
[20] John 14:15–17.
[21] Romans 4:20–21; Hebrews 10:23; 1 Thessalonians 5:24.

Chapter 11: How Do We Do It?

[1] Philippians 2:13 AMPC.
[2] Isaiah 53:4–5 NIV; Matthew 8:16–17 NKJV.
[3] John 19:30 NIV.
[4] John 5:5–9 NKJV.
[5] Galatians 2:20 KJV.
[6] Hebrews 12:2 NASB.
[7] Galatians 5:6 NKJV.
[8] Romans 5:5 NKJV.
[9] Matthew 6:22 NKJV.
[10] 1 Corinthians 5:17 NKJV.
[11] 2 Corinthians 2:14 NASB.
[12] Acts 10:38 NKJV.
[13] John 15:5 NASB.
[14] Luke 17:21 NKJV.
[15] Ephesians 1:3 NKJV.
[16] Proverbs 18:21 NASB.

[17] Ephesians 2:6 NASB.
[18] John 6:63 NKJV.
[19] Romans 4:17 NASB.
[20] 2 Corinthians 5:20 NASB.
[21] Psalm 103:1–2 NKJV.
[22] Hebrews 11:6 NKJV.
[23] 2 Corinthians 5:20 NKJV.
[24] Matthew 28:19 NKJV.
[25] Romans 8:19 NIV.
[26] Mark 16:15 NASB.

Chapter 12: Limitless Possibilities

[1] Romans 12:2 NIV.
[2] Matthew 18:19–20 NKJV.
[3] Matthew 18:20 NKJV.
[4] Matthew 18:19 NKJV.
[5] Romans 5:17 NASB.
[6] Isaiah 26:3.
[7] Psalm 23:5.
[8] Romans 15:13 NASB.

Chapter 13: Taking It to the Nations

[1] Matthew 28:18–20 NKJV.
[2] Romans 8:19 NKJV.
[3] Psalm 18:35 NKJV.

Chapter 14: Sailing the Caribbean

[1] Acts 2:2 TPT.
[2] Acts 2:3–4 MSG.
[3] 2 Corinthians 4:18 ESV.
[4] Romans 8:16–17 NKJV.
[5] Romans 8:21 BSB.
[6] Ephesians 1:23 NIV.
[7] Ephesians 3:10 NASB.
[8] 1 Peter 2:5 NIV; Ephesians 2:22 NASB.

Afterword: It's All about the Wonder

[1] Matthew 18:3 TPT.
[2] Isaiah 45:8 NASB.
[3] Isaiah 9:6–7 NIV.
[4] James 2:13 NASB.
[5] Titus 3:5 NASB.
[6] Romans 8:17 NASB.